Cumbria
MURDERS

Paul Heslop

SUTTON PUBLISHING

This book is dedicated to former policeman, international athlete,
writer and colleague, Arthur McKenzie,
and also to writer and writing course tutor, Nick Cook;
both of whom have been my inspiration.

First published in the United Kingdom in 2007 by
Sutton Publishing, an imprint of NPI Media Group Limited
Cirencester Road · Chalford · Stroud · Gloucestershire · GL6 8PE

British Library Cataloguing in Publication Data
A catalogue record for this book is available from the British Library.

ISBN 978-0-7524-4748-0

Typeset in 10.5/13.5pt Sabon.
Typesetting and origination by
NPI Media Group Limited.
Printed and bound in England.

CONTENTS

AN IMPRESSION OF JOHN HATFIELD

I wish you to be seriously impressed with the awfulness of your situation. Reflect with anxious care and deep concern on your approaching end. Employ properly the short space of time you have to live in preparing for eternity. Hear now the sentence of the law, that you be carried from hence to the place from whence you came, and from thence to the place of execution, there to be hanged by the neck till you are dead. And may the Lord have mercy upon your soul.

These were the words of the trial judge, directed at John Hatfield who was convicted in August 1803 at the Cumberland Assizes, Carlisle, for forgery and avoiding payment of postage charges while falsely purporting to be a Member of Parliament.

On 3 September 1803, Hatfield was 'indulged with a chaise' and, accompanied by a gaoler and his executioner, taken to the place of execution, a small island on Carlisle Sands on the River Eden. A large crowd watched as a small dung cart was placed under the gibbet, and Hatfield climbed the ladder to it. Asked if he wished for any support, he replied, 'No, though my body may appear weak, my mind is perfectly firm.' After thanking his gaoler for his 'indulgence and humanity' during his confinement, he was 'launched into eternity', the first person to be executed in Cumberland in the nineteenth century.

Hatfield's execution had not been favoured by the jury, which declared an unwillingness to let him hang for forgery. They were reconciled, however, because of his heartless conduct towards Mary Robinson, the so-called Beauty of Buttermere, whom he had married while falsely claiming to be the Hon. Colonel Hope, brother of the Earl of Hopetoun, Scotland. Hatfield's remains were interred in a criminal's grave in St Mary's churchyard, outside the city walls.

John Hatfield.

FOREWORD
BY HUNTER DAVIES

Who better than a modern-day copper to investigate what coppers in the past were trying to solve?

Paul Heslop has carried out painstaking research, revisited scenes and examined, as far as possible, all the available evidence before writing about selected crimes committed in what is now the county of Cumbria*. He includes, in detail, the executions of those convicted, and at the end of each chapter offers his verdict, taking into account the testimony of witnesses, the evidence gleaned and, finally, whether justice was done – or otherwise.

Paul Heslop is a retired policeman, with over thirty years' experience, most of them as a detective. Beginning his career on the streets of Newcastle, Paul went on to serve in CID and Regional Crime Squads in two police forces. The 'investigative' experience gleaned over this period has enabled him to reinvestigate and analyse the crimes featured in this book. The result is an interesting and entertaining narrative, inviting the reader to draw his or her own conclusions, just as Paul has done.

Hunter Davies, journalist and author, is a regular contributor to a number of national publications, including the *Sunday Times* and *New Statesman*. He has written over 40 books, including biographies on Beatrix Potter, William Wordsworth and Alfred Wainwright, as well as the authorised biography of The Beatles. His many books include *A Walk Along the Wall*, *The Good Guide to the Lakes*, *The Beatles* and *Football and Me* among others.

---

* The county of Cumbria was formed in 1974, being an amalgamation of the former administrative counties of Cumberland, Westmorland, the Furness district of Lancashire and a small part of the West Riding of Yorkshire. The crimes featured in this book were committed within this area, the present-day Cumbria. Where appropriate, the former county names are used in this book.

ACKNOWLEDGEMENTS

The author wishes to thank staff at Cumbria Record Offices at Carlisle, Whitehaven, Kendal and Barrow, who assisted with the research required to produce this book, in particular Mr Stephen White at Carlisle Library with regard to the archive images reproduced herein; and editorial staff at Cumbrian Newspapers Ltd, the *Westmorland Gazette* and the *Evening News*, Edinburgh, regarding reproduction of images from past publications.

Thanks also to: Mr Brian Parnaby for kindly providing material concerning the murder of his great uncle, PC Joseph Byrnes; Mr Jim McMonies and staff of Cumbria Constabulary regarding information and images relating to Chapter 14; Mr Stewart Lister of Cummertrees; Mr Hunter Davies who kindly wrote the foreword; and, not least, my partner Kate for her support.

Please note that in exceptional circumstances some images have been reproduced without sanction of the original publisher, but only after I have exhausted all means of tracing and identifying them.

ABOUT THE AUTHOR

Paul Heslop joined Newcastle upon Tyne City Police in 1965 (later amalgamated into Northumbria Police). He learned his trade on the beat, supervised by patrol sergeants and shift inspectors, when on-the-street contact with the general public was seen as an essential ingredient in policing. Thereafter, he spent most of his career in CID and regional Crime Squads as a senior detective with Northumbria and Hertfordshire Constabularies, which included investigating serious crime in London and the Home Counties. He retired from the force in 1995 and is now an established writer. He lives in Cumbria.

By the Author:

The Job (Froswick Press, 2000)

The Walking Detective: An account of a walk from Cornwall to Caithness (Froswick Press, 2001)

Old Murders and Crimes of Northumberland and Tyne & Wear (The People's History, 2002)

Bedfordshire Casebook: A Reinvestigation into Crimes and Murders (The Book Castle, 2004)

Hertfordshire Casebook: A Reinvestigation into Crimes and Murders (The Book Castle, 2006)

A DOUBLE EXECUTION

Robert Fox and Philip Tinnaney had little in common, save their lowly position in life. But on a wet and blustery March day in 1827, they would share the moment of death, watched by an expectant crowd of 'several thousand', there to witness the administration of justice in the Border City.

The scaffold was arranged on the roof of the prison wall, facing English Street. At noon the prison bell tolled the 'knell of departure' and they were brought up, two murderers about to pay the penalty for their wicked deeds: Fox, the farm worker from Bankhouse, near Gosforth, who slipped arsenic into his wife's coffee and food, so that she died three days later – following the birth of their child, stillborn, also effectively murdered by poisoning; and Tinnaney, the Irishman who enticed his lover, Mary Brown, into a Carlisle field where he remorselessly beat her to death with a hammer. Now it was their turn to die in the cause of justice. 'I hope the pain won't be protracted,' said Fox. 'Never mind the pain,' replied Tinnaney, pragmatically, 'think of something beyond that.'

The two men appeared, their eyes raised to see the 'engine of death'. Fox, in a state of collapse, cried out to his saviour for pardon. Tinnaney, a Roman Catholic, opted to conclude his devotions on the platform. He knelt in prayer with the priest for nearly ten minutes, as the wretched Fox waited, trembling, forced to listen to the protracted religious mutterings. He was heard to say 'God bless you all' as the executioner stepped forward, tying the legs of the prisoners and pulling the handle that would release the bolt.

The platform did not give way readily, but creaked and sunk a little as the two men, bracing themselves for death, were forced to await their fate. Then it fell, and so did they, together, on that wet and windy afternoon. It was reported that they died instantly, and that afterwards the rain stopped and the sun appeared.

Judgement, without mercy, I own is my due,
I murdered the woman, my confession is true.
With me you may do as you please,
In your great hands you own the keys
Of life or death.
'Tis one request of you I crave,
Leave not this corruption in a grave,
It would be too great honour on it conferred,
Where Christian bodies are interred.
But hang it up on a gibbet high,
Erect between the Earth and Sky.
And let the gibbet rest upon
The ground where the wrong was done;
And in that pasture let it stay
Till it's glutted on by birds of prey,
To be a warning to further ages
In hope to stop such base outrages,
That all who pass that way may see
What human passion brought on me,
That they may tell it with surprise
'Tis life for life did sacrifice.

(Presented to the judge at Assizes by Philip Tinnaney at his murder trial.)

1
A HEART REGARDLESS OF MERCY

Lanercost, 1834

Wilful murder is taking away the life of a fellow creature by malice aforethought. You have to consider whether the violence used rose from an unfeeling disposition and a heart regardless of mercy...

These words, spoken by Judge Baron Parke at the Cumberland Spring Assizes of 1835, could have been drafted with John Pearson in mind. Forty-seven-year-old Pearson was charged with murdering his wife, Jane, in the most brutal circumstances. This was a wicked crime, perpetrated on an innocent woman whose prolonged and agonising death was sufficient to melt the hardest of hearts.

Pearson was born near Haltwhistle, and had been a serial poacher with 'dog and gun' for thirty years, during which he had suffered imprisonment and fines. He admitted that at the age of 18 he had fallen into the 'evil habit of drinking, the mother of many evils'. He had been a gamekeeper, but through drinking and womanising was dismissed. He had married, then joined the army but sought discharge, which was granted after three years. His wife died, leaving five children, four of whom were 'doing for themselves', the other living with a friend. He ended up living and working as a mole catcher at Denton, near Brampton, and married Jane, aged 42. Two months later he murdered her.

The Pearsons lived at Randylands, an isolated house situated alongside the line of Hadrian's Wall, a mile north of Abbey Bridge, near Lanercost Priory. They had lived there for only eleven days when they went for a drink on the evening of Tuesday 14 October 1834, at the Abbey Bridge Inn. Dinah Hodgson, the licensee, recalled their visit. They arrived at about 6 p.m. and left around 8 p.m. John wore a hat, while Jane carried a reticule basket; a small bag made of net with a drawstring. Pearson would later say that he gave Jane his hat to carry also. He drank spirits; she drank no alcohol at all. He was tipsy when they left to walk home; he carrying some coals upon his shoulder, she a bottle loaned to her by Mrs Hodgson containing rum so that

Lanercost Bridge over the River Irthing. John and Jane Pearson crossed this eighteenth-century bridge on their way home to Randylands. (Paul Heslop)

John could continue drinking at home. Taking the rum home was Jane's idea. It was an unwise decision.

Randylands had another tenant, a woman named Rachael Whitehead. She was married, but her husband was away. There were no ceilings in the building, just internal walls, which meant that conversations in adjoining rooms could easily be overheard. When the Pearsons arrived home from the inn that evening, Mrs Whitehead heard their voices before they even reached the house. They were quarrelling. 'He was abusing her very sore and for many things, including of being a whore'. She heard them enter the building and go to their room, where the quarrelling continued.

Then the beating started. As Mrs Whitehead lay in her bed, she could not help but overhear John 'striking and licking' his wife. She told the jury: 'They were very heavy strokes. I heard them more than once, but I cannot say how many times. I was not keeping count. It went on till between 11 and 12. I was awake all the night. I did not take my clothes off. It wasn't very likely I could strip when there was such work carrying on in the other room. Jane called out "murder". That was all I heard her say during the night.'

The next morning Pearson returned to the inn, where he asked Dinah Hodgson for a pint of ale, producing the now empty bottle that had contained the rum. Mrs Hodgson obliged, unaware that Pearson's wife had by then sustained such terrible injuries that she was dying. While Pearson was out, Mrs Whitehead heard Jane call out for a cup of tea. She duly took a cup to her and Jane drank it. She then asked for water, which was also delivered. Mrs Whitehead noted that Jane was lying in bed, naked, and that there was a 'vast deal' of blood about the bed and on her person, including her face. It was the last time she saw Jane alive.

Just after 9 a.m., when Pearson returned home, he showed Mrs Whitehead his wife's gown, telling her she had been in 'idle company' and that she had behaved very badly to him the night before. Later she heard him say to Jane, 'As soon as I have finished then I will finish her,' meaning Mrs Whitehead, who stated that from the time he returned from the inn until 11 a.m. 'he was going on as the night before – striking her.' She told the jury that he had asked Jane 'if she knew the man she was with,' but she made no answer. He said it was 'some person who had followed her out, saw her tipsy and had used her ill.'

Mrs Whitehead left the house around 11 a.m. and chanced upon a neighbour, Sarah Thirlwell, just ten yards from her door. On hearing Mrs Whitehead's account, Thirlwell went up the path to Randylands and looked through the kitchen window in the part of the building occupied by the Pearsons. Inside, she saw a man standing by a bed with a long stick in his hand. His arm was stretched 'full length'. She could not see if anyone was on the bed, nor did she see the man's face. She watched him for three minutes and described him as 'middle sized', wearing a black hat and light jacket. Thirlwell did not know Pearson, but at the subsequent coroner's inquest she saw that Pearson had the 'same appearance' as the man she had seen.

Around the same time, a pedlar named James Barrett happened along. He was walking to Hayton Gate, just east of Randylands. At 100 yards away, he saw a man 'step away' and walk from the house. He identified him as John Pearson, whom he did not know but recognised later at the inquest. As he passed Randylands, Barrett saw 'a person lying before the door'. She was 'quite in a naked state, without clothing at all', he said. He knew her to be Jane Pearson. As he watched, she got up and went inside the house.

Ann Thompson lived at Hayton Gate. After meeting Barrett, she went to Randylands where she found Jane Pearson dead on the bed at about 1 p.m. Pearson said his wife was done, and went outside. Thompson said nothing to him but awaited the arrival of neighbours. When Pearson returned, she asked him 'what had put all the blood on his hands?'. 'It made no matter about that,' was his reply. There was a long stick, like a rake shank, lying in the kitchen. 'It was all blood and hair and sand,' Mrs Thompson told the jury. She also noticed blood in the passage, and 'a great quantity of blood sprinkled

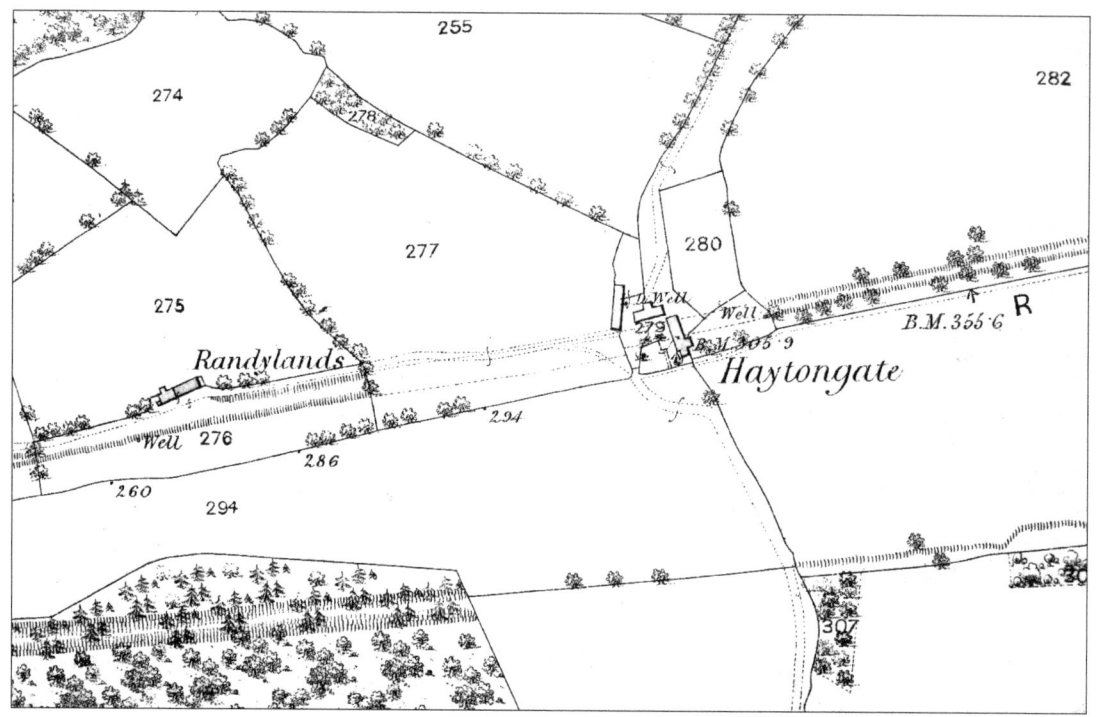

A nineteenth-century map showing the location of Randylands. Note its position in relation to Haytongate, on the course of Hadrian's Wall. (Carlisle Record Office)

on the wall at the bed head where the body was'. She also noticed 'chairs and other things standing disorderly', and that Pearson was 'a little intoxicated' and 'drank from a little bottle'.

Joseph Holmes, a farmer, went to Randylands between about 2 p.m. and 3 p.m. that day. He saw the deceased woman through the window, lying on the bed. He went inside and searched for Pearson but was unable to find him. He then saw Pearson walking along the opposite side of the hedge, whistling and singing, and drinking from a bottle. Meanwhile, those present agreed to lay the body out. Holmes examined the deceased's arms, and different parts of her body. He told the jury, 'I can't describe so horrid it was. I mean by that the body was very much injured. I was shown a large wound on the back of the ahouse was bloody all over. There was hair and blood lying outside the door.'

John Pearson led Holmes to 'a piece of ground' where he said a man had ill-used his wife. It was in the field where the house stood. He said Hugh Hewer knew the man, and that Rachel Whitehead 'knew all about it'. Holmes went to Brampton and brought Constable Robert Sloan to the scene. Pearson was arrested and his clothes and other articles seized. The judge asked Holmes about the place indicated by Pearson, where he said his wife had been ill-used. 'There was an impression on the grass as if some person had been lying there,' said Holmes.

George Gill, a surgeon, carried out the post-mortem examination on Jane Pearson. He found the body 'almost literally covered with contusions and scratches'. There was a wound to the forehead and a contused wound on the back of the head, with a separation of the scalp on each side. This was the cause of death. A stick, like the one produced – about 5ft long and 1½in thick – would have caused it. By the appearance of scratches from hip to head, he considered that Jane Pearson had been dragged along the floor. She could have got up and walked after receiving the fatal blow. Her clothes, the pillow and other articles were produced. There was 'a general expression of horror in the court at the sight of the shocking evidences of the horrid deed'.

Hugh Hewer testified at the behest of Pearson, who had called on him to support his defence. He agreed he had seen Pearson in a field south of Randylands at about 9 p.m. on the evening of 14 October. Hewer, accompanied by his son, had been walking from Garthside to Banks, taking them in a west to east direction. Opposite Randylands he discovered Jane's basket and a man's hat, about seventy yards from the house. Hewer called out, 'Has anybody lost anything?' to which Pearson replied, 'Yes, but stop till I come to you.' Pearson rushed through the hedge and fell over. 'He was very drunk,' claimed Hewer. Pearson then asked 'Where are they?' meaning the basket and hat. Hewer said he would fetch them, and did so. Pearson put the hat on and Hewer handed him the basket. Pearson said the next time he met Hewer in a public house he would 'treat him with a glass' for his kindness.

It was Pearson's turn to have his say. Not on oath, as in those days an accused had no right to testify in his or her defence. Instead, in response to being asked by his Lordship if he had any observations to make, he claimed that when he and Jane had left the inn they were both tipsy, and as he had some coals to carry he gave her his hat, which she carried, along with her basket. He reached home first, but was unable to get into the house because she had the key. After waiting some time in expectation of her joining him, and afraid that someone might 'have taken advantage of her situation to ill-use her', he went back in search of her and found her a short distance from the house in company with a man who was holding the basket in his hand. Hence, he implied, the impressions in the grass, and his hat and Jane's basket being found seventy yards away by Hewer.

Pearson went on to claim that he was in such a state of intoxication that all recollection of anything that might have occurred afterwards escaped him. The next morning, when he found himself in bed with his wife, he immediately got up and left the house to find who had ill-used her the previous night. He then went to the Abbey Bridge Inn, had a drink and then returned home to sit in the kitchen. Noticing his wife was silent, he went up to the bed, placed his hand upon her neck and was surprised to find she was dead. He kissed her and left the house. That was all he knew about the matter, he said, adding that how his wife had come by her death he could not tell but it was not he who had been the cause of it.

This was Pearson's defence against the testimonies of witnesses, especially Rachel Whitehead who had heard the beatings within the four walls of Randylands. The judge instructed the jury to consider whether, on the evidence, John Pearson was the man who had inflicted the violence by which 'the unfortunate woman was deprived of life'. She could not have inflicted the violence upon herself. Explaining manslaughter, the judge told the jury that they must be prepared to make allowance for a man who thought himself aggrieved: corporal punishment might have been an excuse if provocation had been offered, in this case a man who had found his wife in the act of adultery and in a sudden transport of passion had punished her by death.

But there was no proof of infidelity by Jane Pearson, and the treatment she had received by her husband went far beyond 'reasonable', even if his suspicions, if any, had been justified. The jury were told to consider the extraordinary length of time Jane Pearson had suffered, and the instrument by which the violence was inflicted. Pearson had been drunk, although he had considerably recovered by morning when more violence was used. But drunkenness is no excuse for murder, and the jury returned after only fifteen minutes to declare a 'guilty' verdict.

Baron Parke put on the black cap. He told Pearson, 'You have taken the life of your unfortunate wife by means so cruel and brutal as have seldom before been detailed in a court of justice. None can feel pity for your fate. The law says a speedy and incongruous death must be awarded to you, and it is my painful duty to tell you that there is no hope for you on this side of the grave. It remains for me to pass upon you the awful sentence of the law, which is that you be taken hence to the prison whence you came, and from thence on Friday next be carried to the place of execution and there be hanged by the neck until you are dead, and that your body be then buried within the walls of the prison. And may the Lord have mercy on your soul.'

THE EXECUTION

John Pearson had lost the battle, but he had not yet lost the war. On being taken to prison, as the Revd Wilkinson prayed for his soul, Pearson, praying with him, began shaking and 'contorting his body in several ways'. At night he would cry out that his cell was crowded with spirits. He said that he 'durst not sleep alone'. It was a failed attempt to instil the belief that he was insane.

There were rumours that Pearson had murdered his first wife. He claimed she had died of consumption. Given his violent conduct towards his second wife, Jane, who could know what he had done, or what he was capable of?

Randylands today. Just a few stones remain. (Paul Heslop)

He did admit, in a written confession, that his habits had been 'dissolute and depraved'. He owed it all, he said, to 'pride, Sabbath-breaking and intoxication'. Of the murder he wrote the following: 'Being in a state of intoxication, I remember ill-using my wife, but not with the intent to take away her life; although through passion, jealousy and being influenced with drink, I might have influenced on her the wound that caused her death'.

On the morning of his execution, 13 March 1835, Pearson attended a religious service, after which he declared himself 'too full to speak'. Just before noon his arms were pinioned. As twelve o'clock struck he was taken from his cell, saying, 'Christ is my prop – Christ is my prop.' At the scaffold, on top of the wall facing English Street, he trembled as the executioner made the 'last arrangements'. When the cap was pulled over his face he begged for it to be removed so that he could see, but was told this could not be done. Then he was gone, his life taken by the state. It was reported that an 'immense number' of people witnessed the execution.

THE VERDICT

That John Pearson was in control of his actions throughout the entire period he beat his wife may be in doubt: he was drunk on spirits, at least throughout the night, less so in the morning when the beating continued. That he killed his wife cannot be in doubt, and his account of another man 'ill-using' her was a story contrived to save his skin.

The events of that night were heard loud and clear by Rachel Whitehead, who lay alone and fully clothed in her bed, just feet away. She was a victim too. What she must have gone through that long night and into the morning can only be imagined: pity for the poor soul being subjected to prolonged torture; and fear for her own safety, a fear justified when she heard Jane Pearson call out 'murder', and later heard her husband declare, 'As soon as I have finished I will finish her'. There was no telephone to call for help, no neighbour's door to knock on for rescue. She remained in her room, too afraid to flee into the darkness where she might encounter the raging monster.

As for Jane Pearson: she was thrashed mercilessly, time after time, hour after hour. Not with a bludgeon, which might have finished her quickly, but a stick, guaranteed to inflict pain, until, with one blow to the back of her head, she was doomed. Her suffering was prolonged and unimaginable. It is interesting to note that the judge said that 'corporal punishment to some extent might have been an excuse when provocation had been offered'. Thankfully, beating one's wife is one Victorian 'value' that has been confined to history.

After committing murder, Pearson sought to blame another man whom, he said, ill-used his wife when he (Pearson) was too drunk to remember. He strove to be acquitted in court, and when that failed he pretended to be insane. Anything but face the consequences of his wickedness. His end, when it came, was swift and clean. It was more than he deserved.

2
'THAT BAD WOMAN'

Carlisle, 1847

Mary Thompson lived next door to Ann Dixon in Union Street, Carlisle. One Wednesday at the end of May, Mary knocked on Mrs Dixon's door and told her she was so ill she had almost vomited and could scarcely walk. She had great pain in her stomach, she said. Mrs Dixon noticed that her neighbour's face was swollen and her eyes watered. For about three weeks Mary had been complaining to Mary Coxon, another neighbour, about sickness and pains in her head. Mrs Coxon had also noticed her neighbour's face to be 'swelled and altered'.

Later that same Wednesday, Mary returned to Mrs Dixon's house with a piece of veal pie for her 12-year-old daughter, Sarah, and niece, Barbara. It was a kindly gesture that would have unhappy consequences. That day, Sarah had some of the pie for dinner, after which she was 'pained in the bowels' and felt sick. She was off school the following day, when she had more of the pie and was ill again. Mrs Dixon also ate a small piece, after which she was very sick, with pains in the bowels. Barbara, an adult, ate only about a tablespoonful of the pie's crust and meat, but this was sufficient to cause pain in her stomach and bowels. When another neighbour, Margaret McGlasson, saw Mary at her passage door, she saw that her face was swollen, her cheeks were red and she seemed very poorly. Half an hour later she saw Mary at her window, stirring something in a mug.

The following morning, at 8 a.m., Mary called out to Ellen McCormick from her bedroom window, asking her to go for Mrs Coxon, as she was ill. Ellen duly fetched Mrs Coxon and the pair went in to see Mary, who was lying on her bed fully clothed, complaining of a pain in her stomach, a burning heat in her throat and vomiting. She told them that her face felt 'as if it had been nettled'. When she vomited into a small tub at the bedside, Mrs Coxon noticed that it had a green and yellow appearance. At Mary's request, Mrs Coxon took some oatmeal from a closet and placed it into a gill of water, which Mary drank thirstily. Mrs McGlasson arrived and together they undressed Mary, then sent for John Thompson, her husband, who was at work at Richardson's timber yard. When he arrived shortly afterwards, he said Mary had been ill all night, through bile in the stomach, he thought. Mrs Coxon noticed Mary was frequently taking the oatmeal in water. Indeed, she mixed it for her three times. She told Thompson to fetch a doctor.

The 'doctor', John Mortimer, was in fact a surgeon. On hearing Mary's symptoms, he told Thompson there was no hurry for him to call on his wife. He arrived at the house at noon and prescribed 'effervescing draughts and hot fomentations'. Mary said she felt a great deal better, but Ann Dixon, who also visited her that day, found her very ill. She also observed the oatmeal and water in the pint pot.

Around 8 a.m. on Friday morning, Mrs Coxon again called on Mary, who was in bed with the same complaints. She sent for her husband, who was told to fetch the doctor again. Mary said she felt so ill she thought she would not get better. Mrs Coxon remained with her for an hour and a half, and when she left the doctor had still not arrived. When he did arrive he found Mary sitting on the edge of the bed, 'Her countenance exhibited stupor, great depression and great anxiety.' He gave her opium, and again ordered hot fomentations. John Thompson was present throughout. When Mrs Coxon called again that evening, Mary said she was 'rather better'. Her pint pot containing oatmeal and water was at her bedside.

Around 8 a.m. on Saturday morning, Mrs Coxon sent her 12-year-old son, Robert, next door to enquire about Mary. He found her lying on the bed, 'her hand on her elbow and her knees drawn up.' She was not wearing a nightgown or a nightcap. 'Her person was exposed,' Robert told his mother, adding that he thought Mary was asleep. For this reason Mrs Coxon did not go next door. If Mary was not actually dead at that time, she was when John Mortimer called at the house three-and-a-half hours later.

Mortimer estimated that Mary had been dead for three hours. The bed was in 'great confusion', with the covers pushed to the foot. He did not think there had been any struggle in death (an amazing conclusion). He saw a tub in the room containing fluid, and buckets containing vomiting matter. There was an iron pot on the drawers, which contained boiled bread and water. He sent for Mrs Coxon, who noted that Mary wore a shift, which was drawn up as far as her knees. Her nightgown and cap were 'thrown off and on the floor'. There was a chamber pot under the window, covered with an old hatbox top. Pint pots and gill pots stood on a box, one with a little meal and water in it. Mortimer gave strict instructions that none of the vessels should be thrown away or washed out. We can assume he must have had certain suspicions at that point, albeit belatedly.

Another neighbour, Jane Dalton, was sent to fetch John Thompson who, as usual, was at work. 'You must come home directly,' she told him. 'What's the matter, is she worse?' he enquired. 'Yes, she is dead,' Jane replied, breaking the grim news. 'It's a queer thing she's dead,' Thompson uttered, 'she told me she was a good deal better this morning.' Thompson duly went home. He wanted 'things emptied', but Mrs Coxon told him the coroner would have to be brought, and that the doctor had specified that nothing be thrown out.

Carlisle in 1847. (Carlisle Record Office)

At 1.30 p.m. Mary Rook came to clean the house. Mrs Coxon told her not to touch the chamber pot or a dish containing vomit. Ms Rook duly washed the house and cleaned crockery, and two dirty basins. She left the chamber pot and other vessels as she was bid. Eleanor Graham also called. She saw oatmeal in a basin with a spoon in it, and another basin with what looked like boiled rice and water. There was a small tub with something in it 'like gruel settled at the bottom', and green water above. She also told Thompson that nothing was to be put away, by order of the doctor. At this point we might enquire into the conduct of John Thompson. From Wednesday through to Saturday of that week, when neighbours attended to his wife as best they could, where was he when she had suffered so? Other than brief periods when he called at their two-roomed dwelling, two places mainly: at work at the timber yard, or consorting with a woman named Margaret Kane.

Mary Thompson died a lingering and dreadful death. No cause had yet been established, but it soon would be. The surgeon, John Mortimer, had given strict instructions that the vessels containing oatmeal and vomit were not to be cleaned, and Mary Rook complied. But Thompson didn't, for as soon as he had the opportunity he emptied them and washed them out. But there was other evidence that would incriminate him in his wife's murder: the contents of her stomach, and certain powders found in his pockets, sent for analysis by 'medical men'. They found that Mary had been systematically poisoned with arsenic, and as result of this Thompson, as prime suspect, was charged with murder by administering arsenic into the veal pie that Mary innocently gave to Ann Dixon, her next-door neighbour, and into the oatmeal she repeatedly consumed in the belief that it was doing her good.

John and Mary Thompson were married at All Saints Church, Newcastle upon Tyne in 1827. They had no children. In 1846 they moved to Carlisle, taking up residence in Union Street. Thompson was then 42 years of age. It seems their marriage was normal enough, until, that is, Thompson met Mrs Kane at Edward McBride's beer shop the previous September, after which he became a regular. They knew him by the name John Peel, as others did. Thompson, or Peel if you will, falsely said his wife had died six or seven years before, at Maryport. His liaison with Kane, which lasted eleven months, was nothing short of scandalous in eighteenth-century Victorian England. She accepted him as her lover in the belief that he was not a married man.

John Thompson stood trial for murder at the Cumberland Assizes in August 1847. He pleaded not guilty. In his opening address, Mr Sergeant Wilkins, prosecuting, told the jury that after Thompson had met Margaret Kane, he started neglecting his wife, telling Kane she was dead and buried. Kane had been a widow for nearly eight years, and when she met Thompson she had lived in Sowerby's Lane, Botchergate. She confirmed meeting him at McBride's beer shop, when he said his name was John Peel and that he was a widower. They met again, when he came up to her room, and he continued to visit her, 'persevering in courtship' and talking of marriage. He sometimes stayed with her through the night, having 'criminal intercourse', until about two or three o'clock in the morning. Later he took a room in Irving's Court and she moved in.

In April, Kane received a letter which read:

This is to certify that Elizabeth Thompson, wife of John Thompson, died, and was buried in the parish of Crosscanonby on 14 August 1841 (or 1842).

John Brown, clerk.

Being illiterate, she showed it to Thomas Hind who lived next door, and he read it for her. But, on the day after Mary's death, Kane told Thompson she had heard it was his wife who had died. He said, 'No, it never was.' He had 'owned' her as a wife at the inquest, she said. He denied it, saying he was 'put up to own her for the sake of things.' He continued to deny that Mary was his wife, and still did. Kane admitted 'intercourse' with Thompson up to the time of Mary Thompson's death, even though she had discovered his real name, and that he was married. Ann Magnay, Kane's sister, went to live with her at Irving Court, and said Thompson called at one o'clock on the day after his wife's death. She asked him if it was true his wife had died. 'She was no wife of mine, she was the landlady,' he told her.

There were other witnesses to Thompson's nocturnal activities. Eliza Hoyle lived with her husband on the same floor as the Thompsons. She knew Thompson was in the habit of coming home between 3 a.m. and 4 a.m. in the morning. This started just before the previous Christmas. He would knock on his front door and be let in by his wife. Another neighbour, Mary Halfey, had got up between 5 a.m. and 6 a.m. on the day of Mary's death. She heard someone on the stairs and opened the door to see Thompson on the street, 'as if to go to work'. He was carrying his breakfast tin. That same morning Thomas Drinkwater, a millwright at Richardson's yard, saw Thompson arrive a few minutes before 6 a.m. Drinkwater said there had been 'sad stories' about him having connections with a woman named Margaret Kane. All lies, claimed Thompson.

This, then, was the picture: John Thompson, a married man, was having 'criminal intercourse' with a widowed woman, Margaret Kane, to whom he purported to be called John Peel, a widower. He would leave her in the early hours to go home, to be admitted by his wife; and then he would leave again shortly after to go to his work at Richardson's yard. He had secured premises in Irving's Court, paid for by himself and Kane. His liaison with Kane had continued thus, including throughout those final days in May, despite his wife's grave illness, and even after her murder.

At 2 p.m. on Saturday 29 May, Thompson went to the police office to give notice for an inquest. He told Sergeant Haugh that he had got up early, made his breakfast, given his wife a cup of tea and gone to work as usual. Sergeant Haugh located the coroner and then went to summon a jury. (How procedures have changed.) At 6 p.m. that evening the police, including Superintendent Sabbage, went to Thompson's home, together with the coroner and medical men. The officers made a search and took possession of the contents of Thompson's pockets; a powder-like substance was placed in packets, sealed and given to the doctor. At some point during the search Thompson went next door to Mrs Dixon's house. Jane Bunting, a neighbour, saw him there. He asked her what Mr Sabbage and all those doctors could be doing in his house. 'Very likely viewing the body,' she said. 'What was there to view?' he asked. 'It's to ascertain the cause of death,' she told him. He asked if they could tell what the cause of death was. 'Yes, by opening it,' was the reply. He said he was sure he had not given her anything that would do her hurt.

Dr Robert Elliott MD performed a post-mortem examination on Mary Thompson. He reported 'a body healthy in appearance in all respects, except the stomach, which had redness and inflammation, with many ulcerations about the size of split peas'. The intestines were inflamed. He reported, 'beyond all doubt we found twenty-eight grains of yellow arsenic from the stomach alone, and thirty-six grains of the same from a portion of the intestines. In all, sixty-four grains of yellow arsenic'. He had no doubt this was sufficient to cause death. Thomas Elliott, a surgeon, carried out a Reinsch's test, a chemical process. He concluded that Mary Thompson had consumed arsenic in repeated doses.

Burial certificate: 'Mary Thompson, age 43 years, of Union Street'. (Carlisle Library)

Arsenic was a commodity freely available in Victorian England. Anyone could visit their local druggists and buy it over the counter – just as John Thompson did. John Fisher was an assistant at a veterinary practice, which had a druggist's store in Scotch Street, Carlisle. About three weeks before Mary Thompson's death a man came in and bought one-pennyworth of arsenic. Fisher served him, and wrapped the arsenic up in two papers on which he wrote 'Arsenic – Poison'. The man wanted it for poisoning rats, he told the court, a common enough reason then. About a week before Mary's death the man returned and purchased another pennyworth, which was wrapped and labelled as before. On 4 June, when Fisher attended the inquest, he thought he saw the same man in the room. It was John Thompson. He wasn't certain, he said. But William Graham was. Graham was a post office clerk who had been in the druggist's shop on the first occasion the man came in and bought the arsenic. Giving evidence at the assizes, he looked at Thompson and affirmed that he was the man. He too attended the inquest and identified Thompson, 'standing among 15 or 16 persons'.

On 7 June PC James Boardman went to Thompson's house where he took possession of a small bag of oatmeal from a cupboard. It was found to contain arsenic. Following the post-mortem and analysis of substances found in the house, Superintendent Sabbage arrested Thompson the following day. Following what the officer had heard about the veal pie, a search was made of a midden behind his house, but nothing was found. Prosecuting counsel told the jury: 'That she died from arsenic, there can be no question. That the veal pie she partook contained arsenic you will believe. That the oatmeal she was in the hourly habit of taking was thoroughly impregnated with arsenic is equally clear. Arsenic was found in the pockets of the prisoner's working jacket. He bought arsenic for a reason that was false. How came the arsenic into the oatmeal? Who was living near the poor woman? Thompson had fixed his affection on another. His wife was a stumbling block. He had the means, the opportunity, the motive.' He ruled out suicide. 'Would she have destroyed herself by inches?'

Defending, Mr James challenged the notion that Mary Thompson had died from arsenic poisoning administered by her husband: the medical men had calculated different figures; there was no proof of poison in the stomach; the dust in Thompson's pockets might contain arsenic from the iron amongst which he worked; someone entertaining an ill will towards the deceased might have mixed the arsenic in the oatmeal with the poisonous substance; none of the veal pie was recovered, so it could not be analysed; there was doubt about the identity of the man who purchased the arsenic; Thompson had been an affectionate husband for twenty years. Could the jury believe that for such a woman as Margaret Kane Thompson would deprive his wife of life, seeing that she had not been a bar to the gratification of his wishes? It was for the jury to decide whether they would, on a tissue of 'prejudiced testimony', consign to death a man who, it was possible, was innocent of the offence imputed on him. 'There was a cloud of doubt and the prisoner ought to have the benefit.'

When the jury returned, after twenty minutes, they found Thompson not guilty of mixing arsenic with the veal pie, but guilty of mixing arsenic with the oatmeal. The judge told him that he had provided himself with the means of getting rid of his wife, 'whether for the purpose of disposing of a woman who had become burdensome to you, or because her presence interfered with your lawless connection (with Kane)'. His wife had consumed ten times the quantity of arsenic that would produce death. 'You saw her wasting away with lingering torture, producing death by the most cruel means that could be adopted to satisfy your depraved condition.' Even when his wife was in the agonies of death, he was seeking the society of another woman. 'It was your hand that administered the poison. It was your will and intention that caused her death.' Thompson listened with stoic indifference to the inevitable sentence before leaving the dock, exclaiming, 'I am as innocent as you are, my Lord.'

THE EXECUTION

On the day after his conviction John Thompson confessed his guilt to the prison chaplain. He had wanted to marry 'that bad woman Kane', and he expressed the wish that his confession be made public. He asked to see Kane, but this was refused. He asked to see her children, and this was granted. When they came to his cell he took the little girl upon his knee and told her to tell her mother that it was she who had brought him to his untimely end but that he forgave her. Poisoning his wife was her fault, then.

They erected the gallows facing the street on the night before the execution – a night when Thompson slept more soundly than at any time since his conviction. He may have confessed, but there was little public sympathy for him. No attempt was made to get up a petition to have his sentence commuted.

Saturday 21 August 1847 was market day. Five thousand of Cumberland's good citizens were reported present, seeking to secure good vantage points from which to witness Thompson's demise. Just before noon the Sheriff 'demanded the body' and Thompson was pinioned. He said he died in peace and forgave everyone, and hoped everyone forgave him. Whether they did is doubtful. As the bell tolled he was led to the scaffold, accompanied by the governor, the chaplain and the executioner, John Calcraft. His step was firm as he took his position beneath the beam of the gallows. He asked that his hair be turned back from his eyes, as it prevented him seeing the crowd. After shaking hands with the gaoler and the chaplain, he said, 'May God bless you,' the last words he would utter. When Calcraft pulled the bolt the wretched man struggled at the end of the rope before finally succumbing.

THE VERDICT

John Thompson perpetrated the wickedest of crimes against someone he should have loved and cared for: his wife. He administered arsenic in small doses over a period of about three weeks, so that she wasted away, dying in agony and alone. That the surgeon, John Mortimer, did not think she had 'struggled in death', is astonishing. He seemed slow to respond to requests that he attend her address. Surely the dreadful state Mary Thompson was in merited more positive action.

Not that anything could have saved her once John Thompson embarked on his mission of death. Why did he do it? If he wanted to win the affections of Margaret Kane so desperately, surely he could have simply moved in with her. But it was not so simple in Victorian times. Margaret Kane wanted to be 'respectable', which meant she wanted an unattached male and Thompson knew it. He sent her a certificate, purporting to prove his wife's death and burial some years before. But his wife was very much alive. It must have seemed so much easier to simply get rid of her.

So, a little at a time, Thompson mixed arsenic into his wife's oatmeal. The one thing she believed might make her better was the very thing that was poisoning her. And all the while her husband spent his time with another woman, creeping home in the dead of night to his lonely, dying wife. It was reported that when they hanged him he struggled at the end of the rope. If his death was an agonising one, it was but a mere trifle compared to his wife's prolonged suffering at his hands. He deserves not a shred of sympathy.

3

AN ENGLISHMAN'S HOME

Thursday 17 April would have dawned as uneventful as any any other day for the good folk of Walton, three miles north of Brampton. But the day would become very much eventful when 12-year-old Mary Ann Graham went to make her customary delivery of milk to the parsonage. Just before 8 o'clock, as she reached the gate, she saw a man lying on the ground. He lay on his back, with his hat close to his head and his stick nearby.

Mary Ann went to fetch Mary Nixon. Mrs Nixon, having seen the man for herself, went to the parsonage where her knock was answered by Ann Glendinning, a servant of the Reverend Joseph Smith. She told Miss Glendinning to tell Mr Smith about the man, which she did. The reverend, who was unshaven and not yet properly dressed, accompanied the two women to the gate. Mrs Nixon asked him if he thought the man was dead. 'Sure enough, he is dead,' he replied. 'We must fetch somebody,' said Mrs Nixon. Mr Smith returned to the house, and Mrs Nixon went to seek William Taylor, who went to the parsonage gate. Like Mr Smith, he also formed the opinion the man was dead. Joseph Forster, a farmer, thought the man might have had a fit, while others who had gathered thought it possible he had galloped to the gate on horseback and been thrown over it. (The man's horse was found wandering about, still wearing bridle and saddle.) Ann Glendinning and Sarah Blacklock came from the house, followed by Smith, now fully dressed and shaved. Glendinning told them she knew the dead man, but could not name him.

Forster took some letters from the man's pockets and handed them to Smith, who read out loud that they were addressed to Mr Armstrong of Sorbie Trees. The same name was found in the man's hat. Smith bent down to examine the body and found a hole in the man's coat. It was on the right upper breast. He then declared, 'I've been the death of him,' and when Forster lifted the undercoat, which was also holed, he said it again. 'The man's shot himself,' said William Taylor. 'No, Mr Smith has shot the man,' said Forster. The small crowd fell silent until someone said the body should be moved, and it was removed to the inn.

The Revd Smith had indeed shot the man, just before midnight, twice in fact, with a revolver he kept in a drawer. The man had staggered 45 yards from the front door of the house, where he was shot, to the gate where Mary Ann Graham had found him. And now Ann Glendinning remembered she had been a servant of the man's father, eight or nine years previously, when she had lived in the same household. She confirmed his name: William Armstrong.

Armstrong was a landed farmer of Sorbie Trees, Roxburghshire, Scotland, eighteen miles from Walton. He was 37 years old, married with two children, and described as 'an affectionate husband and good father'. On 16 April, he travelled on horseback to Brampton to make arrangements for the purchase of property. It was market day, and he met up with acquaintances and shared a few drinks, 'but not in any quantity to damage his faculties or to obscure his intellect or reason.' At 9 p.m. he and William Elliot of Bewcastle mounted their horses to ride home. On a bright, moonlit night they rode north. At Cambeck Bridge they were joined by Thomas Richardson. The three men visited an inn where they remained until about 11 p.m., when they left, taking the road towards Walton, the way home for all of them. Armstrong galloped ahead and was not seen again until Mary Ann Graham discovered his body at the parsonage gate the following morning.

The inquest into Armstrong's death was held before the coroner, William Carrick, by which time there was speculation about the purpose of Armstrong's visit to the parsonage. It seems he may have been seeking to hire the services of Ann Glendinning, his father's former servant. But why call at nearly midnight? Well, he was passing, and he'd been drinking all afternoon and again in the evening, so maybe he didn't care about the time. But there were reports that he had been on terms of 'improper intimacy' with Miss Glendinning, which she emphatically denied.

When in Brampton, Armstrong had declined the invitation of friends to remain in town all night, saying he had an appointment to meet the Duke of Buccleuch's hounds early the following morning, at Canonbie. Was he thus making himself available for a midnight tryst with Miss Glendinning? A messenger who arrived on her husband's horse, meanwhile, informed his wife of her husband's death. When told that he had been shot at the Revd Smith's front door, she remarked, 'Had he but askit him what he wanted there, William wad hae gi'en him a civil answer.' Sadly, her husband was never given that opportunity.

We must look to the Revd Smith himself for the explanation of events that night, which he gave at the inquest, saying 'everyone must sympathise with me in my unfortunate position.' His youngest child had become restless, he said, 'screaming with much violence'. Steps taken to quieten him interfered with retiring to rest. At almost midnight he was left alone, his wife having gone to bed. He then took 'his usual round' – seeing that all the windows and

The gate at Walton parsonage. (Paul Heslop)

shutters were properly fixed. 'I was removing some shirts which were in front of the fire in the south-east room when I was very much alarmed by a great knocking.' It came from the study window, he said.

'I became exceedingly agitated, and went into the study when I saw the bar of the window was not fixed. I went forward partly in the spirit of self-defence but more under the influence of fear, and with the view of showing some timid bravado I made a noise in putting down the iron bar to intimidate any party outside. I was under the impression that it might be some vagrants, sailors and other mendicants, quite dreadful to look upon, who had molested me on former occasions, and had spoken to me through the window more in the way of intimidation than asking charity. Without waiting for further noise I took a revolving pistol out of a drawer and snatched up a lantern. I became so utterly unnerved and agitated, so devoid of all self-possession and judgement, I went forward, alone as I was, drew the bolt of the front door, shot back the lock loudly and drew back a sliding guard chain, and opened the door, when I at once discharged the pistol two or three times without aiming at any object, more in the hope of alarming than killing.'

His actions were proof, he said, of how 'utterly wanting' he was in self-possession by exposing both himself and the house by opening the door 'and like the moth rush to my own destruction.' He went on, 'I may mention that the moon was on the southern side, and cast a shadow on the north-west side of the house (where the door was). These circumstances, combined with my lantern, which casts more light on the person who holds it than it throws forward, made it impossible for me to distinguish any object.'

He went on: 'The reason I provided myself with a pistol was the painful anxiety of mind occasioned by the Frimley murder (alluding to the recent shooting of a curate at Frimley, Surrey) and not being possessed of any strength to cope with any violence, and living in a house with females and children, accessible at all sides, I felt it my duty to have firearms to make an alarm in case of danger.' He had tried another pistol, but found he could not hit anything with it. After firing the pistol (on the night of the shooting) he came in, secured the door and began to feel concern that he had shot somebody. He thought it his duty to go outside and, with lantern in hand, he did so 'in fear and trembling'. He saw nothing and came inside, thankful that no injury had been sustained by anyone.

William Elliot, who had earlier told the inquest that he and Armstrong had ridden together to Cambeck Bridge and then towards Walton, again testified. As they neared Walton, Armstrong told Elliot he had 'seen an old acquaintance', Ann Glendinning, who was living at the priest's house and he was going to call on her that day as he would like to have her again as a servant. His servant, also called William Elliot, confirmed Armstrong's intentions. Armstrong had told him he had seen Ann Glendinning the previous week, and that he had 'treated her with a glass'.

Dr John Graham carried out the post-mortem examination of William Armstrong. There were three wounds on the trunk, caused by two bullets. One was a small wound near the edge of the right shoulder blade. The bullet had entered the body, passed through the soft part of the armpit and made its exit by the shoulder joint. About 4in below was a small penetrating wound caused by a pistol bullet. Dr Graham explained graphically the route this bullet took through the vital organs of the chest, before lodging between the spine and the sternum. This was the fatal shot.

The coroner told the jury, 'Gentlemen, I cannot subscribe to the doctrine that a man should seek to be excused for taking another's life, acting under a nervously timid state of mind, having lost all self-possession, having become void of all prudence and discretion. It would be a most dangerous rule indeed were we to allow such an excuse to justify a man in so extreme an act as taking another's life.' The jury found the Revd Smith guilty of manslaughter. It would be for another jury, at the assizes, to decide the same or otherwise. Smith was so overwhelmed he 'cried and sobbed like a child, subsequently sinking into a state of imbecility of mind'.

At the trial the following August, the public was eager to see the 'unfortunate clergyman who was about to occupy the degrading position

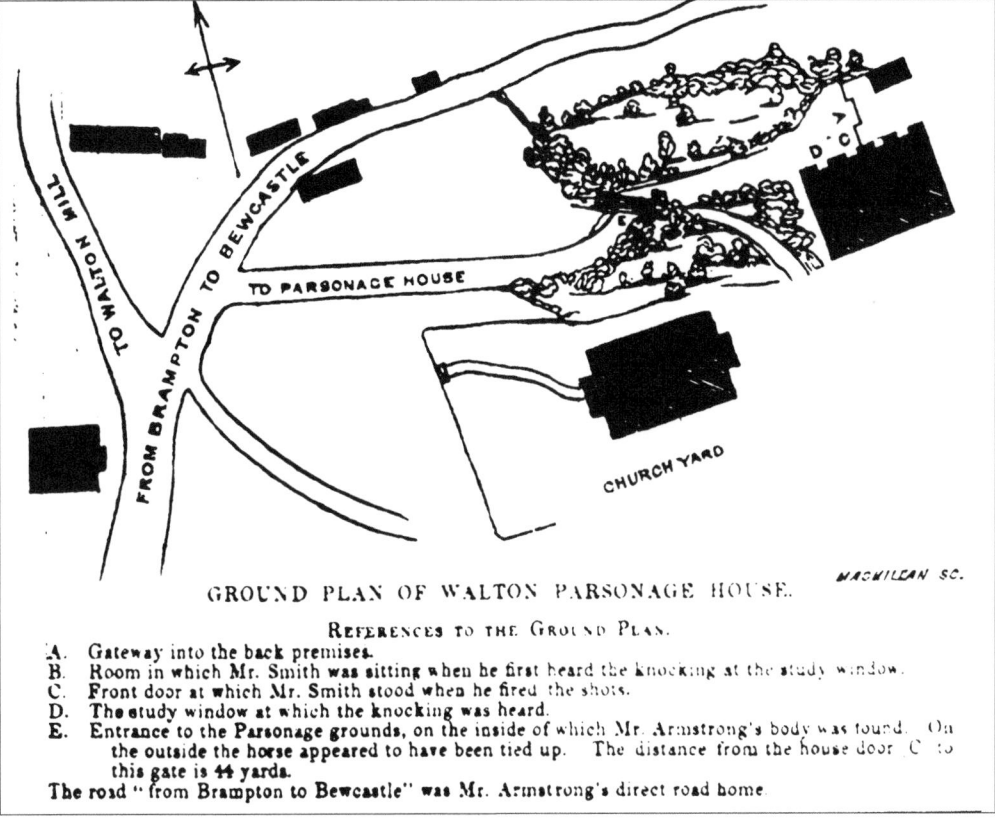

GROUND PLAN OF WALTON PARSONAGE HOUSE.

REFERENCES TO THE GROUND PLAN.

A. Gateway into the back premises.
B. Room in which Mr. Smith was sitting when he first heard the knocking at the study window.
C. Front door at which Mr. Smith stood when he fired the shots.
D. The study window at which the knocking was heard.
E. Entrance to the Parsonage grounds, on the inside of which Mr. Armstrong's body was found. On the outside the horse appeared to have been tied up. The distance from the house door C to this gate is 44 yards.
The road "from Brampton to Bewcastle" was Mr. Armstrong's direct road home.

Plan of Walton parsonage. (Carlisle Journal)

of prisoner at the bar'. Baron Platt presided. As the case was called Smith climbed slowly up the steps of the dock, and with downcast eyes shunned the steadfast gaze of the crowd. He was permitted to sit with his wife, a concession seldom, if ever, granted someone charged with homicide. Was the jury thus being invited to consider with sympathy the case against the man of God? Mr Temple, prosecuting, outlined the facts. They were the same as heard at the inquest. 'The law does not allow men to deal so wantonly and carelessly with the lives of their fellow creatures. If you are not of the opinion that the prisoner did not make use of that care and caution which were necessary and prudent before taking steps which might end in fatal consequences, you will think him guilty of manslaughter.'

Ann Glendinning described the house and gardens of the parsonage. There were trees and shrubs, and inside the gate thick shrubbery on the south side extending up to the house. There were more trees near the gate and to the north side of the drive. She said her employer was 'very much terrified', there being no man in the house except himself. Constable John Foster asked Smith why he had fired at the man without speaking. 'I would have suffered much

Walton parsonage.
(Carlisle Journal)

THE PARSONAGE HOUSE, WALTON.

before I would have fired,' said the constable. Smith said he thought 'they were going to break in upon him'. 'He changed colour when he was talking to me,', said PC Foster.

Thomas Harrison, a gunsmith from Carlisle, said Smith had bought a pair of pistols the previous November. He had brought one back, wanting a larger one which he was given. He said he too had heard of the Frimley murder, and that 'he sold a great many pistols after that time, and cleaned and loaded a great many more.' Joseph Smith wasn't the only one living in apprehension after events in Surrey. The coroner, Mr Carrick, told the court of Smith's statement, which had been taken down in writing at the inquest. There followed discourse as to its legality. It could not be given, said the judge, as it was made under oath. Since the prisoner was not permitted to testify, his account of events was not heard at the trial.

Mr James, for Smith, accepted Smith was responsible for the death of 'the unfortunate gentleman'. He did not imagine for one moment the jury, 'as Cumberland men, who have always been noted for generosity and good feeling', would allow themselves to be biased. He went on: 'The law of England is that a man may use firearms or other weapons in the defence and protection of his life and property during the hours of the night, if his house, which we Englishmen are wont to call a castle, is assaulted.' Mr Smith lived in an exposed and lonely place; his house was separated from the others in the village. 'A horrid murder takes place in this country (at Frimley), a minister of the gospel in the dead hour of night has his life ruthlessly and savagely taken away; the newspaper columns are filled with details of daring robberies and burglaries committed day after day. Is it astonishing that Mr Smith should purchase a pistol for the protection of himself and those near and dear to him? Can anybody doubt that the terror that pervaded all classes of society extended itself to Mr Smith, a man of exceedingly nervous and timorous disposition?'

Armstrong Obelisk in
Ettleton cemetery.
(Paul Heslop)

Mr James invited the jury to ask themselves what anyone should do if, even late at night, they wished to speak with the minister. The visitor that night went to the window. 'Is there not a door? Is there no knocker or bell? Do you imagine for a moment if there had been a knock at the door Mr Smith would have opened it and fired the pistol? Certainly not! He would have enquired what was wanted. So terror-stricken was he, so deprived of judgement, he places himself in the position of greatest danger: he throws back the bolt, opens the door and fires three shots. The instant the shots are fired the door is slammed.

'Do not be led away with the notion that because Mr Armstrong was not a robber there was no excuse for Mr Smith. Ann Glendinning had lived with him and his father and might have wanted to be in their service again. But what an hour to go on such an errand! Being intoxicated, he rides to the gate, dismounts and walks up to the house, but instead of knocking at the door he rattles the windows to the terror and consternation of Mr Smith. The deceased had no business there at that unreasonable hour, and his death was brought about by his own imprudent act.'

The inscription on the tablet reads:

'In this spot, near which rest the ashes of his forefathers, is interred William Armstrong, of Sorby Trees, who to the great grief of the neighbourhood was shot without challenge or warning by the Rev Joseph Smith, incumbent of Walton, Cumberland, on the night of Wednesday the 16th April 1851, in the 38th year of his age.

In affectionate remembrance this monument is erected by a numerous body of friends on both sides of the Border, as a tribute of their respect for one whose mainly straightforward and generous disposition gained him the love and esteem of all who knew him'.

It was after 10 p.m. by the time the judge finished summing up. One can imagine the courtroom: flickering oil-lamps, gaunt spectators' faces, the hapless vicar sunk into his chair, his face buried in his hands as he and his distraught wife awaited the jury's verdict. It took forty-five minutes. 'Not guilty,' said the foreman. The Revd gentleman was assisted from the dock and, accompanied by his wife, left the court. Today, a tall granite obelisk stands in Ettleton cemetery, on a bleak hillside near Newcastleton, 'in affectionate remembrance' of William Armstrong, erected by his friends on 'both sides of the Border as a tribute of their respect'.

THE VERDICT

Why did William Armstrong call at Walton parsonage that night? To enquire about hiring Ann Glendinning, whom he knew was a servant there, and with whom he was acquainted? Or were they more intimately involved and, if they were, did she tell him that everyone in the household retired before 11.30 p.m., and that if he were to call just before midnight and rattle the window she would join him in the darkness? If so, it was Armstrong's wretched luck that Smith had not retired; he would have thought it was Glendinning who was opening the door. But whether they had or had not conspired to meet that night is irrelevant when considering whether Joseph Smith was culpable. He was a timid man, weighed with the responsibility of protecting the occupants of the household, so much so he purchased two pistols. But did he have the right to possess a gun for 'protection'?

Well, yes he did. As defence barrister, Mr James, told the jury, 'A man may use firearms in the defence and protection of his life and property during the night.' That William Armstrong was not a burglar didn't matter. What did matter was that Joseph Smith believed his life and property were threatened. He was not guilty of any crime at all, according to the verdict of the jury.

But it is not the verdict here. Surely 'belief' meant that he had cause to believe that the nocturnal visitor was hostile. He could have fired a warning shot through a window, or called out. Or not opened the door at all. One of his own parishioners, perhaps in some unforeseen family crisis, might have sought his counsel, even so late at night. Was that a light still burning? Might it be Mr Smith hadn't retired yet? Such a caller may have knocked at the window, so as not to disturb others in the household; he would have heard Smith drawing back the bolts and seen him in the doorway, holding his lantern – only to be shot for his trouble.

Whatever the reason Armstrong called at the parsonage, he was not a criminal. He was either there legitimately, or for the same reason that has motivated men since time immemorial. Maybe his judgement was impaired by alcohol, but he did not deserve to be shot dead, at a parsonage of all places, and Joseph Smith, no matter how frightened, ought not to have discharged his pistol so readily at the spot where someone might be standing. He was guilty of manslaughter at least.

4

NOTHING BUT DOUBT AND DIFFICULTY

Kirkland, 1854

The fields around Kirkland, near Ennerdale Bridge, seldom witness much in the way of human activity. A farm worker or two, or a passer-by on a lonely footpath. Such was the case on a quiet Saturday in November 1854 when a stranger appeared, a man who may not have expected to be noticed let alone stirred anyone's curiosity. But he was noticed, if only because his presence was so unusual.

The first to see him was 12-year-old Joseph Braithwaite, who was cutting turnips in a field at about 9 a.m. The man was in the next field, about 100 yards away. He wore a dark coloured, square-tailed coat and light trousers. About half an hour later Joseph Unthank, a farmer, left his house at nearby Hunter How to go shooting, when he saw a man approaching from the west, in a field with no path. Unthank lost sight of him, but soon after he saw the same man going towards Lanceray (or Lancelow) Bottom, a rough pasture with whins (grassy banks). The man was wearing a dark jacket and a cap.

At about 10 a.m., Joseph Kitchen, a farmer, was working in a field called Hall's Acre, cutting a thorn hedge, when he saw a man standing about 150 yards away in the middle of another field. A footpath ran through Hall's Acre and the man was standing about 40 yards from it, looking towards Hunter How, a position from which he would be able to see anyone coming up the path. He wore a dark cap and coat, a dark waistcoat and light trousers. As Kitchen worked along the hedge, the man moved out of sight, into the depression leading to Lanceray Bottom. Quarter of an hour later, Kitchen saw the man again, still looking towards Hunter How. A quarter of an hour after that Kitchen saw a second man approaching, on the path. This was about 10.45 a.m. He lost sight of this man and carried on working. Twenty minutes later he went to the field gate at Lanceray Bottom and saw a hat lying about 4 or 5 yards from the path. He then saw the body of a man, a yard or so from the path, lying face down. The man's throat had been cut.

The body was warm, and the wound, which went almost entirely across the man's throat, was still bleeding. There was blood all over the man's face, waistcoat, shirt and neckerchief; and more blood on the grass, and a pool of blood about 3 yards away. The ground nearby was scratched and grazed, as if there had been a great scuffle. Kitchen thought the dead man was the second man he had seen, walking up the path.

Meanwhile, another farmer, William Johnstone, of Gill Farm, saw a man running along the top of the field, stooping down and looking back over his shoulder. His description matched that of the first man seen by Braithwaite, Unthank and Kitchen. Around noon, or shortly after, young Joseph Braithwaite, still cutting turnips, saw the man he had seen earlier walking 'very fast', then running in a westerly direction behind some hedges, stooping as he ran. Then Edmund Watson, a farmer of Salter Hall, over a mile from where the body was discovered, saw a man behind a hedge in a stubble field, heading towards Wath Brow. He was dressed in a dark shooting jacket and cap and appeared to be wiping perspiration from his forehead.

Kitchen raised the alarm by telling John Jackson, who told Wilson Jackson. All three examined the scene at Lanceray Bottom. They found the dead man's pockets had been turned out, and they picked up silver coins, which were strewn about the body. John Graham, who also attended, found the haft of a razor a few yards away. John Jackson found the blade of a razor. There were no distinctive footprints. They took the body by cart to Hunter How. Hearing of the murder, Edmund Watson, who had seen the man hurrying towards Wath Brow, searched for footprints in the field. He was unable to find any complete ones, except for some 'heel and neb' marks, including one in particular which he considered identifiable. He placed some small stones around the mark and a larger one on top to protect it.

The dead man was identified as Isaac Turner, aged 58, of Cleator. Turner had worked for over twenty years for Lindow's, iron ore merchants, who had a drift mine on Kelton Fell, to the east of Kirkland. The drift had been open for ten or twelve weeks, and Turner was foreman to a workforce of four men. It was his routine to pay them, at the mine, every other Saturday, which he did by either walking or riding from Cleator, via Ennerdale Bridge and Lanceray Bottom. On the Saturday in question, 4 November, he had walked as far as Ennerdale Bridge, where he was obliged to change the two £5 notes he carried so that he could pay the men their wages.

At 9.15 a.m. Turner arrived at William Parker's shop at Ennerdale Bridge, where he changed a £5 note for three sovereigns and silver. He then called at the Dog & Gun public house, where Ann Tyson changed the other £5 note. She gave him three half sovereigns and the remainder in silver. He stayed five or ten minutes, had a glass of gin and then left, bound for the drift at Kelton Fell, less than two miles away.

The stranger – almost certainly the murderer – had been seen. That he knew Turner's movements, and known he would have been carrying men's wages on that particular Saturday, seemed likely. Where could the police start? In fact, where they started isn't known exactly. What is known are the events that

Lanceray (or Lancelow) Bottom. (Paul Heslop)

transpired at a house not far from the scene of the murder: the home of Amos Munroe and his wife, Jane.

The Munroes lived in Kirkland with their children and Amos's half-brother, 18-year-old Thomas. Both Amos and Thomas had worked the nightshift at Lindow's drift throughout the week, including Friday night through to Saturday morning. As usual, they both went home afterwards, arriving at about 6 a.m. On the Saturday in question, however, Thomas did not go to bed. Instead he had breakfast, washed and left the house sometime between 8 a.m. and 9 a.m. Thomas returned around 6 p.m. that evening, as news of the murder swept like wildfire around the community. He sat behind the door, spurning the warmth of the fire despite being wet through from heavy afternoon rain. He remained there for twenty minutes before going to the bedroom he shared with two of the Amos children, from which he emerged ten minutes later and left the house.

If Thomas's conduct on the day of the murder didn't attract suspicion on Saturday, it seems Jane Munroe's attention was drawn to her brother-in-law the following morning. Thomas and Amos were out, and when Jane went to make Thomas's bed she saw his dark brown coat hanging up. She took it down and noticed blood on the sleeve. She showed it to her brother, John Hellon, who happened to be in the house. She did not know where Thomas's trousers and shirt were, but he had a box in the room, which was locked. She hung the coat back up in the place she had found it.

Knowing of the murder, Jane Munroe would have been mortified to discover the bloodstained coat. Perhaps she then also reflected on Thomas's strange behaviour the previous evening when he sat, wet through, away from the fire. In any event, she sent John Hellon to fetch John Dickenson, a local magistrate, and soon afterwards the two men found Thomas in the garden, having his hair cut by the blacksmith, William Rigg. Rigg told them that on the day after the murder Thomas had asked him to cut his hair. Cutting hair was hardly part of a blacksmith's skills, but Munroe asked him again that afternoon, and produced a pair of scissors. The reason, the prosecution suggested at Munroe's trial the following February, was to change his appearance.

Dickenson asked Thomas Munroe if he could have the shoes he had worn the previous day, and to look into his box. Munroe gave him the shoes and with some hesitation consented to Dickenson's latter request. From the box, Dickenson took out a dark, square-tailed coat, 'much marked' with blood – the same one found by Jane Munroe that morning. He also saw a bloodstained cap. He looked under the bed and found a basket with old rags in it. He made a thorough examination of the room, even turning the mattress up. There was no sign of trousers or shirt.

That Sunday evening, Superintendent James Clarke arrested Thomas Munroe on suspicion of murder. The officer found a knife in his jacket, and the key to his box, which contained 18s 4d. He found a basket under the bed containing a miner's jacket. There was still no sign of trousers or shirt. On the way to Whitehaven, Munroe said, 'I can clear myself. I was at Wath Brow Top public house yesterday at eleven o'clock. There were two women in the house who waited on us. I was with a man from Ravenglass, Bob Robinson.' Clarke knew the pub to belong to Mrs Ann Fisher. He drove directly to it and asked Mrs Fisher if Munroe and a young man had been there, as Munroe had described. 'No,' she replied. She had never heard of anyone named Bob Robinson. Her daughter, also Ann, denied seeing 'two young men' the previous morning.

Thomas Munroe gave the police an account of his alleged movements on the day of the murder. All was verified save for his whereabouts at the time of the murder. Apart from his assertion that he was in the Wath Brow Top pub at 11 a.m., which he could not substantiate, he had called on his Aunt Bella at Arlecdon, at 1 p.m. At about 4 p.m. he called upon another aunt, Mrs Munroe, who had a shop at Arlecdon. He was looking for his half-brother, William. When his aunt told him about the murder, Thomas replied, 'It's a bad job.' She told the police he had been wearing a dark square-tailed coat, a dark blue cap and light trousers.

Superintendent Clarke came into possession of the clothing and shoes seized by John Dickenson. The shoes he took to Salter Hall, where Edmund Watson had so diligently covered the footprint made by the stranger. Clarke made impressions with the shoes, alongside the footprint. He formed the opinion it corresponded with the left shoe. This 'evidence', though honestly produced, was hardly satisfactory. Meanwhile, although the police had a bloodstained coat and cap, no trace had yet been found of the shirt and light-coloured trousers Thomas Munroe had worn on the Saturday.

Then came a breakthrough. Amos Munroe said he'd found a basket under Thomas's bed at 6 p.m. on the Monday evening. It contained a pair of trousers and a shirt wrapped up in an old jacket. This was after the magistrate, John Dickenson, had looked under the bed and found a basket which, he said, had not contained trousers or shirt, and after Superintendent Clarke had found a miner's jacket but, again, no trousers or shirt. After Amos found the trousers and shirt, Samuel Lindow, his employer, called at the house. The moment he arrived Amos gave the clothing to him. The trousers looked as if they had been washed, the shirt was so wet 'you might wring it'. Lindow gave the trousers and shirt to Superintendent Clarke. Meanwhile, the police produced a number of witnesses to identify Thomas Munroe as the stranger seen before and after the time of the murder. In the gaol yard, Munroe was placed with eight other men, all wearing similar caps and coats to his. Kitchen, Johnstone and the boy Braithwaite were asked, separately, if they could identify the man they saw. Kitchen first identified the wrong man, and being given a second opportunity selected Munroe. Johnstone identified him, and then admitted he had seen him on a previous occasion at the smithy. Braithwaite picked him out without hesitation, but only by his dress and size. He had never seen the man's face. The procedure was certainly not in keeping with today's stringent identification rules.

Two surgeons named Bateman and Fidler examined the body of Isaac Turner. They stated his throat had been severed, not with a razor, but with a blunt instrument. The wound was caused when a knife was thrust in two or three times on the left side and drawn right round down to the spine, 'dividing the windpipe'. A sharp pointed instrument, such as the knife found in Munroe's possession, might have been used. Mr Turner had been attacked from behind. Once his throat had been severed he would not have been able to cry out.

The broken razor was not the murder weapon. Nevertheless, Henry Steel, who was in service with Munroe at Sellafield for a year, said Munroe had been in possession of a razor, which, if true, might suggest it was his that was found at the scene of the crime. William Yeat, a farm servant at Sellafield, confirmed Munroe had worn a square-tailed coat and also told them that he and Munroe had 'bled a cow' before Munroe left employment there. Munroe himself had explained the blood on his coat by 'bleeding a cow'. Much of the prosecution's case rested on the bloodstains. There were plenty to analyse, but unlike today no means of 'grouping' which would assist in ruling a suspect in or out. Munroe said the blood on his clothing was cow's blood. Could an expert say if it was human blood?

Alfred Taylor, professor of chemistry and medical jurisprudence at Guy's Hospital, London, examined the razor, knife, jacket, cap and a pair of trousers. First, he examined the razor and clasp knife. He was not able to say conclusively that there was blood on either. He carried out 'chymical tests' on sample pieces from the coat and cap to establish if the spots and stains were blood. This involved the application of nitric acid, heat and ammonia. All red colours will stand a boiling temperature; heat congeals the serum of blood, as it had in this case. When ammonia is added to blood it undergoes no change of colour; in all other red colours ammonia changes the colour to green. The spots were blood, concluded Professor Taylor. As to it being human blood, he formed his opinion from microscopic measurement. The small globules in a human being are, in diameter, 3,500 to an inch. The globules in a cow are, in diameter, 4,200 to an inch. Of all mammals, the hare, rabbit and dog come close to human in size of globules, as to be hardly distinguishable. So was it human blood or not? His professional belief was that it was, but he added, 'I would not pledge my oath it was human blood.' Hardly a conclusive reply to condemn a man to the gallows.

Defence counsel addressed the jury: 'What evidence was there that the prisoner, Thomas Munroe, was the murderer?' The identification was unsatisfactory, the preserved footprint could have been made by any one of hundreds of shoes, Professor Taylor said he thought the blood was human but then 'could not swear to it', and even if it was, it could not be proved to be Isaac Turner's. The razor may or may not have been Munroe's; more likely the murder weapon was a knife. Munroe had a knife, but which young man didn't? 'There was nothing from beginning to end but doubt and difficulty.'

Which leaves Bob Robinson, with whom Munroe claimed to have been in the Wath Brow Top pub. Where was his testimony? A vital witness, neither prosecution nor defence called him. A man's life was in the balance: if Robinson had corroborated Munroe's story there would surely have been cause for reasonable doubt, sufficient for acquittal perhaps. It seems the responsibility for Robinson's attendance, along with the cost of a solicitor, was Munroe's, and he had not the means to pay. The judge threw his weight behind the testimony of Professor Taylor. 'We may be sure that these gentlemen (experts) who look into microscopes are not wrong. They can measure with great accuracy indeed...' The jury found Munroe guilty of murder, but recommended mercy 'on account of his youth and previous good character'. Asked what he had to say, Munroe replied, 'My lord, I am as innocent as the child unborn. I hope the Lord will bring to light the man that did the horrid deed, that every eye may see that I am innocent.' Passing the inevitable sentence, the judge told him he had 'justly been convicted' and would 'die an ignominious death upon the scaffold'.

THE EXECUTION

Even while incarcerated in the condemned cell, Thomas Munroe protested his innocence. No one came to visit him: no friends, no family. A magistrate, a man of God and his gaolers, strangers all, were his sole comforters. But he did something to cause serious concern about his conviction: he made a written statement to the prison chaplain. His 'confession' (edited), reads thus:

> I was never in the public house at Wath Brow Top with Bob Robinson on the day of the murder. I was at the places where witnesses swore they saw me, but I neither committed the murder nor did I see it committed. I was there by appointment of Amos Munroe. Amos asked me if I could keep a secret, and refused to tell me unless I would promise never to divulge it. I promised I never would. Amos told me he was going to murder Isaac Turner, and asked me to assist him. I said I would not do such a thing. Amos promised to give me the whole of the money he got from Turner if I would go with him, as he wanted to be foreman in Isaac's place. Amos asked me if I would go across the fields towards the spot where the murder was committed, and then run across the fields towards Cleator, so that people might think that some person from that neighbourhood had committed the murder. Amos must have worn my clothes, as I had not them on at the time. I was on the side of the Gill towards Cleator, and I saw my brother, Amos Munroe, on the opposite side of the Gill towards the whins. Amos told me that Isaac Turner would pass the place about 11 o'clock. I was to look at my watch and start to run about 11 o'clock. I have no doubt the witnesses saw me when I was running. I made up the story about Bob Robinson in order that I might clear Amos and myself. I would have confessed before, but expected a reprieve and I was anxious not to fetch my brother into the scrape. I did not think they would hang one so young as I am.

If what Munroe said was true, it would have great bearing on the case, not least the need for another trial, that of his half-brother, Amos. Representation was made in London to present this new information to Sir George Grey, the Home Secretary, submitting that there was a case for 'extending time for a few days'. This seemed reasonable, but Sir George said he could not interfere.

As usual, thousands turned up to watch the public execution on Tuesday 13 March 1855. Munroe received the summons without any indication of fear. As the bell tolled and the procession moved towards the gallows, the chaplain prayed 'in a slow and solemn voice': 'I am the resurrection and the life, saith the Lord...' The *Carlisle Patriot* reported, 'Most sorry we were to see the great number of women: young women and old; children – bits of things that could scarcely toddle or talk – were permitted to share in that sad spectacle of human misery. Even mothers with infants at their breast watched the last agonies of the expiring boy'. Munroe stood firm and turned his eyes from the crowd as Calcraft drew the cap over his head and adjusted the rope. Asked if he had any last words, Munroe grasped the hand of the chaplain and said, 'All I have to say is that the statement I made to you is the truth. I shall die with the name of Jesus on my lips.'

THE VERDICT

'Nothing but doubt and difficulty,' said counsel. He was right, in so many aspects of this case. Lack of certainty about Munroe being identified as the man witnesses saw in the fields at Lanceray Bottom; lack of injury after 'a great scuffle' between the killer and the deceased; no proof that any of the stolen money was found in his possession, nor that he wore the bloodstained coat on the day of the murder. Professor Taylor would not 'pledge his oath' that the blood on Munroe's coat and cap was human. The trousers that had been washed were apparently placed under Munroe's bed after he was arrested. Was there really enough evidence to condemn a man to the gallows? There was not – at the trial.

But Thomas Munroe's 'confession', made after his trial, suggests that he played some part in events. If, as he alleged, he acted in collusion with his half-brother, he was still guilty of murder – but so was Amos. Amos and his wife were both arrested in the course of the investigation. Did the police treat them as suspects, or merely lock them up until they had the statements necessary to put the blame squarely on the shoulders of Thomas? We do not know. What is clear is that Thomas Munroe's 'confession' merited investigation. Maybe the Home Secretary didn't consider events in far-off Cumberland worthy of his time. In this regard, justice was neither done nor seen to be done.

Could it be possible that Amos was the killer? He had motive: the money, or to become foreman at the mine. At the time of the murder he said he was in bed at home; his wife, no one else, corroborated this. Jane said she found Thomas's bloodstained coat; did the police regard this as proof that he was the killer? This was, after all, the point at which he slotted into the frame. On her testimony Thomas was ruled in and Amos ruled out. And wasn't the summing up by the judge somewhat biased? 'We may be sure that experts who look into microscopes are not wrong.' It was as if the result of the blood test was crucial. It was not. The result would prove it to be animal blood or human blood; but it would not prove it was the victim's blood. The jury recommended mercy for Thomas Munroe. He was 18 years old. This was a brutal and premeditated crime, but was hanging him in front of thousands of spectators any less brutal than the murder of Isaac Turner?

5

A BARBAROUS MURDER

Embleton, 1860

It was after 5 p.m. when Mrs Isabella Fearon got home, on Monday 26 March 1860. She expected her knock to be answered by Ann Sewell, the maidservant at Beckhouse Farm. She was surprised when no one came to the door, and just as surprised to find it locked, and even more so when she looked through the window to see the fire was not lit. So she went and fetched Sarah Earle, a servant girl at the Boyes' farm, to climb through the kitchen window and let her in. What Sarah Earle found inside Beckhouse Farm that late afternoon would shock not only the neighbourhood and county but would even find its way into the newspapers in far-off London.

There, in the lobby, lying face down in a pool of blood with a table knife loosely clasped in her left hand, was Ann. So surprised and shaken was Sarah that, instead of opening the door to the waiting Mrs Fearon, she climbed back through the window to tell her of her grim discovery. Mrs Fearon told her to fetch George Cass, a farm worker who was brush harrowing with horse and harrow in a nearby field. On the way she encountered Joseph Clarke, a neighbour, and told him about Ann. Clarke went at once to the house. Meanwhile Cass, on being told the news, told Sarah she 'must be mistaken.' Nevertheless, he took his horse to the stable, where he lingered before Clarke saw him and told him to come to the house.

Access to the house was at the rear by either of two doors. One, the main entrance, led down a step to the lobby, where Ann was found; the other opened to a washhouse, which was secured on the inside by a wooden bar that slotted into a staple. Mrs Fearon told Cass to climb through the window. There was no need, he said, as he could get in through the door to the washhouse, a strategy he employed when he arrived at the house late at night. He took a piece of iron from the top of the door, and opened the door with it. He went inside and opened the other door from within. Clarke went inside, where he found Ann. Her neck was cut on the left side. He took the knife from her hand, and then he and another neighbour lifted her into the parlour where they 'happed her up' with some bags. Clarke told Cass to fetch his master, Thomas Fearon, and tell the coroner. Cass got on his horse and galloped off in the direction of Cockermouth.

Beckhouse Farm. (Paul Heslop)

Twenty-six-year-old Ann Sewell was from Lamplugh. She had started work with 'batchelor statesman' Thomas Fearon at Beckhouse the previous November. She and Cass, 24, lived in with Fearon and his widowed mother, Isabella. Two day-labourers, James Elland and James Boak, also had access to the house, which stood among fields (as it does today) about quarter of a mile from St Cuthbert's Church. It appeared that Ann had committed suicide: there was no sign of a forced entry, the two doors being secure, and there were no footprints on the soft earth beneath the windows, with the exception of Sarah Earle's. The house had not been ransacked. No property was missing. There was no sexual violation.

But Ann had not committed suicide. As Dr Dodgson testified at the inquest, and again at the assizes the following August, her injuries were not self-inflicted. At the post-mortem examination, he found a deep wound that 'commenced near the back of the neck and terminated near the centre of the chin'. It was 7in long and 2in deep. The carotid artery and jugular vein were 'divided', and the spinal cord was cut across. There was a slight wound near the front of the neck, 'merely through the skin'. There were cuts to her hands. She had been murdered, but by whom and why? We must look at events as they unfolded that March day.

Thomas Fearon and his mother had left the house that morning for Cockermouth market, where she remained while her son went about his business. Ann would have busied herself 'seeing to the beasts' and doing household chores, while Cass and the two labourers worked in the fields. At about 9.30 a.m. John Robinson, the parish clerk, called at the house and borrowed a pail and mop from Ann, which he used to clean a hearse, a task which would take five-and-a-half hours. Another visitor was Jane Atkinson, the mother of George Cass's illegitimate child. She had travelled from Whitehaven to ask him for the maintenance he had not paid. Cass told her to go to Cockermouth and see Fearon. Later, Ann would cook dinner for herself, Cass, Elland and Boak, as well as five men and a boy from Keswick who had called to collect corn, and Joseph Gibson, a labourer. After dinner, it seems the Keswick men left first, followed by Boak, and then Elland before 2 p.m. Gibson left shortly after, leaving Ann and Cass alone in the house.

Just after 3 p.m. Mary Ann Thompson walked down the road to where John Robinson was cleaning the hearse. As she passed the farm she heard a dog barking, but saw no one, including Cass, who would have been visible enough if he was at work in the fields. She spoke briefly to Robinson, who locked the church before going up to the farm to return the pail and mop. He knocked on the door, but no one answered. He tried to open the main door, but found it locked. He went to the stables where he saw Fearon's mare, the same horse Cass would have used to work in the field. He left the pail and mop in the stable.

At about 5 p.m. her employer, Mr Boyes, told Sarah Earle to see about some hurdles (sheep pens). She went into the field where Cass was now working and asked him where they were. In the stack-yard, she was told. Earle thought he did not seem to be his usual self, 'as though he were frightened'. She went and got the hurdles, noting that both doors to the house were shut. It would be half an hour later when Mrs Fearon asked her to climb through the window.

Without any apparent motive, the police found it difficult to identify a likely suspect. Of the nine men who had been with Ann for their dinner that day, five of them (and the boy) were quickly eliminated as they were sighted in a pub on the way home. The murderer had left the house and secured the door behind him. This would presumably be the washhouse door which, as Cass had demonstrated, could be opened from outside with the iron bar. Cass, however, may not have been alone in knowing how to open and close the door. Elland, Boak and Gibson were all familiar visitors. Suspicion fell on James Farrish, a miner. He was Ann's sweetheart, and a love letter from him was found in her belongings. There were whispers that she was pregnant by him, and that they had quarrelled. But Farrish had a cast-iron alibi: he was at work at Green Gill Mine that day.

Superintendent Brown saw Cass two days after the murder, on the 28th. He asked him if he had seen any strangers about the farm on the Monday afternoon. Cass said he had seen John Robinson (who had washed the hearse) at one of the doors to the house. It was when he was repairing the brush-harrow in the field. Cass showed Superintendent Brown where he had been standing and the officer drove a stake into the ground there. Brown observed that a person could not be seen at either door from this point. Meanwhile

Elland, and a man named John Thomlinson, said that on the evening before her death Ann had told them she had found a half-crown. She had not had the opportunity to spend it, yet there was no money in her possession when she was found.

On 6 April the police arrested Cass and Elland on suspicion of murder. Elland was quickly released when Cass, who was taken to Cockermouth, told Inspector Douglas that he wished to make a statement under caution. It amounted to a confession, although some of it was clearly untrue. Edited, it reads thus:

She made me mad, you know. She was in the passage, or lobby, coming out of the front door leading into the yard opposite the stable. She wanted me to do something with her caulkers (clogs). As I would not she began to call me. She had a knife in her hand. I was standing between the stable door and the house door, and she threw the knife at me, and the haft catched me on the left cheek. I took it up and threw it at her. She was standing within a yard from the door in the passage, and it struck just about there (pointed to his Adam's apple). She ran to the bottom of the passage. 'Oh dear,' she says, 'come and put me away altogether.' She begged and prayed of me twice or three times to do it. I took up t'knife and came a stroke across the left side of her neck. She put her hand up to the left side of her face and said it did not seem to go far enough. I gave her a second one when she asked me. She stood a little bit, then she dropped. I came into the kitchen and I took the knife and thought I would wash it and then I rued – I would not; I put it into her hand. Then there was a drop of blood about the size of a halfpenny (pointing to his waistcoat).

John Robinson came to the door. I was in the back kitchen washing my waistcoat. I stepped aside till he went away into the stable, and then went home. I went into the kitchen and out of the front window into the orchard. I got my mare out of the stable and when I got her into the field she would not stand until I got the gear on. She went galloping back into the fold. I brought her back and yoked her. I saw nothing more till Mr Boyes' girl came. When I got home Mrs Fearon told me to go in at the front window. I said I could get in at the back door. I had got in many a time, and I opened the door for the mistress with that piece of iron.

After we had gone to bed, I went upstairs into Ann Sewell's room. Her and me was down at Cockermouth one night and she wanted to get some things. She had forgotten her purse, and she asked me if I had any money, and I said I had half-a-crown if that would do aught to help her, and I lent her it. As I had lent her the half-crown I thought I would have it back. I looked into her box and there was a little bag they hang over their arms. I found a purse in it. I put the eighteen-pence in the purse in my pocket. Then I groped her frock pocket, as I thought there might be something in it, and there was half-a-crown. I put that in my pocket. I did not know what to make of the sovereign. I owed our folk a sovereign, and I was over home on Wednesday night and I left the purse and sovereign with my mother. I spent the half-crown. I had eighteen pence left, then I ran out of 'bacco, and sent for another ounce. I had fifteen pence left. Sarah Dixon, the person I sent for the 'bacco, only gave me three halfpence instead of threepence. I had given her a sixpence out of the eighteen pence. That is all...

With this confession George Cass incriminated himself, at least as far as manslaughter. If he was to be believed, Ann Sewell invited him to cut her throat. The slight wound to her neck may have been caused, as Cass alleged, when he threw the knife at her. He didn't sneak into her room for the money until the middle of the night (he said), so it appears robbery was not a motive. His confession was secured with astonishing speed. Inspector Douglas said Cass elected to make the statement within half an hour of being taken into custody. (There were rumours that a policeman entered Cass's cell dressed in a sheet and waving a lantern, purporting to be Ann's ghost and scaring him into confessing. As if!)

Now the police had identified their killer, they had to build a case. Joseph Thompson, a labourer, was just the man they were looking for. Asked by Superintendent Brown if he could 'rake up anything in his mind about Cass', Thompson said that the day before the murder he and Cass were sitting on top of Ling Fell, smoking their pipes, when Cass declared, 'Joe, I will cut our lass's throat, the damned lazy bitch.' Another man, Henry Maclean, said that

Ann Sewell's grave in Embleton churchyard. (Paul Heslop)

he was with Cass at Mary O'Brien's house, Cockermouth, on Shrove Tuesday. When Cass had wanted to 'put his hand' on one of the servant girls, Maclean said he had a 'canny lass (Ann) in the house with himself', and that he need not come to Cockermouth for a sweetheart. Cass said, 'She would be fitter killed or drowned' and could 'find it in his heart to see her throat cut and would think no sin of it'. They were drunk at the time. Mary O'Brien's house was a place of prostitutes, said defence counsel.

At the Cumberland Assizes in August, Cass's eyes filled with tears when his mother was brought to the witness stand. She said, 'George came over on the Wednesday night, the 28th. He gave me a sovereign, a purse and a half-crown. I returned the half-crown. He owed me the sovereign and I kept it. Next morning I had the purse in my pocket and let his father see it and he put it in his pocket as he was going to Loweswater.' Cass's father, John, 'a respectable looking man', said, 'I got a purse from my wife on 29th March. I put it in my pocket. I kept it until I was going to work when I got some gravel in my shoe. I took out my knife and the purse came with it. I dropped it and stuck my stick in it, thrust it down and lost it.' He later went with Superintendent Brown and recovered the purse, which lay about 10in deep in the moss. Elizabeth Hetherington, who once worked as a fellow servant with Ann at Camerton Hall, identified the purse as Ann's.

Mr Price, for Cass, did not dispute that Cass had killed Ann Sewell. The law, he said, was that every killing was *prima facie* murder; but not if there were circumstances to lead a jury to believe it might be manslaughter. He spoke of 'the frailty of human nature and rage that can render a man deaf to the voice of reason'. There was not deliberate malice in this case. The prisoner was an irritable man, brought into contact with a 'handsome girl perhaps inclined to flirt a little, and perhaps knowing his temper she was inclined to rally him'. She had held him at arm's length, while other men were about. 'She made me mad, you know', Cass said in his statement. Mr Price asked the jury to consider the consequences of a murder verdict against one of manslaughter. 'Punishment will follow a conviction for manslaughter, but life may be granted to make atonement, to spend in penitence and remorse for his crime.'

The judge said it was not for the jury to consider 'consequences'; it was for them to consider their verdict based on the evidence. 'If he (Cass) was acting on a request from Ann Sewell to cut her throat, that was murder.' The jury agreed, but were 'anxious to recommend mercy'. The judge told Cass, 'You will have time to make your peace with God,' whereupon he 'choked his utterances' before continuing to pass sentence. It cannot be easy sentencing a man to death.

A puzzling feature is that Cass's clothes must have been bloodstained; yet he only accounts for washing one garment, his waistcoat. What happened to his shirt and breeches? It seems he may have hid them in the barn, behind an old boiler. There does not appear to be any record of the police finding this vital evidence. Did they look – or did someone remove them? One also wonders about James Elland. There was, it seems, a strange encounter on the afternoon of the murder between him and Boyes, who was sitting on the jury at the inquest. As Boak was testifying, Boyes interrupted him, saying he was coming down from Ling Fell at about 3.30 p.m. when he heard footsteps and saw Elland coming from the farm, carrying something above his head wrapped in straw. They did not speak, and after following him for a few yards he lost sight of him. No mention was made of this at the trial. What had Elland been doing? Was he carrying Cass's bloodstained clothes? If so, he would have been in some way connected with the crime.

Carlisle Gaol (right). Built in 1827 on the site of a previous prison, and rebuilt in 1869, it closed in 1922 and was demolished fifteen years later. Victoria Viaduct and the railway remain. (Carlisle Record Office)

Ann Sewell was buried in St Cuthbert's churchyard, Embleton. A humble servant, she would never have expected such a grand headstone. The inscription, protected from the elements, reads: 'Sacred [to] the memory of Ann Sewell, whose life was terminated by the hand of an assassin while in the discharge of her humble duty...'.

THE EXECUTION

George Cass was hanged on Tuesday 21 August 1860. A new scaffold had been erected behind the projecting angle of the gaol wall; it was lower than before and set farther back so that the drop could not be seen from the street. The crossbeam was visible, but only from Devonshire Street and Lord Lonsdale's statue. An estimated 4,000 people gathered to watch, many from the west of the county.

Awaiting his fate, Cass made two further confessions. In the first, he said his quarrel with Ann was not about repairing her clogs, but about the half-crown he had lent to her. He had upbraided her about it, she had 'retorted'; he had rushed at her and caught her as she was making her escape through the outer door. He dragged her down the passage and cut her throat. The second, perhaps, was the truth:

I was smoking my pipe after dinner, and about three o'clock Ann Sewell began to call me ugly names and told me about my bastard child. She said everybody hated me. She then threw some cinders at me out of the grate. I jumped up and got hold of a knife, which was on the table. I got hold of her by the shoulders and cut her throat. After I saw the blood I wished I had not done it. I thought I could not mend it, so I cut her throat again. I then went upstairs and changed my shirt and breeches. I washed my waistcoat. I then went into her bedroom and looked in her box. There was a purse. I took it. There was a sovereign and 1s 6d in it. I gave the sovereign to my mother.

Cass was visited on the day of his execution by his family, but not his mother, as he thought she could not bear it. As the hour approached, the High Sheriff demanded the body. Cass was pinioned, and the usual procession to the scaffold took place: first the chaplain, followed by Cass and hangman John Calcraft, with a turnkey on either side; then the High Sheriff, the Under Sheriff, the Governor, and finally the Sheriff's chaplain. Cass's step was firm as he uttered the words, 'Lord Jesus, receive my spirit.' Every pair of eyes was turned upward as Cass appeared on the scaffold. Calcraft placed the white cap over his head, and the chaplain prayed for the condemned man. At three minutes past the hour the bolt was drawn and he disappeared from view. The crowd filtered away, except for a few who waited the hour until the body was cut down. Cass left all his worldly goods, £8 in unclaimed wages, to his illegitimate child.

THE VERDICT

George Cass murdered Ann Sewell. He admitted as much in three written statements. But why? Because she asked him to repair her clogs? Because she refused to pay him back the half-crown she owed him? It was probably neither of these reasons. His third and final statement is probably nearer the truth: that they quarrelled when they were alone in the farmhouse, that she taunted him and under provocation he cut her throat.

However, the true story of events leading up to that fateful afternoon may be more to do with unrequited love. One sees a picture of two young people of the opposite sex living closely connected lives in that remote farmhouse. Cass may have made overtures; Ann would have rejected him. With no outlet for his sexual and amorous demands, Cass found solace in Mary O'Brien's brothel, a place that provided sex but not love. Ann had told her erstwhile fellow servant, Elizabeth Hetherington, that Beckhouse was dull and that she intended to leave. She was unhappy there, and maybe she was fed up with Cass too. He was a ticking time bomb waiting to explode – as he did that fateful afternoon.

6

THE KILLING OF
OLD JANE

In the mid-nineteenth century Durran Hill, Carlisle, was an isolated and lonely place, where the road from Botcherby to Harraby crossed the railway. Jane Emmerson, the crossing keeper, would routinely emerge from her cottage to open and close the gates across the highway. Her cottage was situated to the east of the crossing, on the north side of the tracks, about twenty-four yards from the gates. Jane was a 72-year-old widow, an 'old woman', as the Victorian press described her. She may have been old, but age had not wearied her. After her husband died six years previously, she had taken up his duties at the crossing, a job that commanded lots of time in what today would be classed as unsocial hours.

Thursday 21 November 1861 was typical enough, as the mineral train from Newcastle, driven by Thomas Thompson, passed by at 9.40 p.m. Thompson noticed a light in the cabin by the crossing, although he didn't see Jane, who would have opened the gates across the highway once the train had passed. Just after 11 p.m., when George Hind made his way to the railway sheds to start the nightshift, he saw that the gates were in odd positions: the two on the north side were wide open, hard back against the hedge, as was the south-east gate, while the south-west gate was straddled halfway across the line. Yet at 4.20 a.m. John Atkinson was able to drive his train through the crossing, as the gates were correctly positioned.

At 5.50 a.m. William Blaylock, a platelayer, found Jane lying about four yards from her door, 'quite dead'. She was wearing her usual clothes, including a 'clout hat'. He saw that blood had poured from her mouth and nose. He hurried to the engine sheds to fetch James Carruthers and Edward Peel, and together they went to the cottage where they found the door open. Inside, some drawers had been disturbed, and the bed had not been slept in. They carried Jane into the house, noting the body was 'a little warm and quite limber'. Then they went into the garden and found the wicket gate open. They also found a slasher – an implement used for cutting hedges. It had a shaft about 4ft long, and a long iron blade, which had blood, hairs and glass particles on it. They noticed three panes of glass in the cottage's window had been broken, although no entry had been made at that point due to the iron framework.

The police attended the scene at 7.30 a.m. They included Chief Constable Dunne and Inspector Alexander Taylor. It should be borne in mind that these were the days before fingerprint technology, blood grouping analysis and forensic aids, such as DNA. What would be required to crack the case was good policing, and that is what happened from the start of this investigation. They had two mysteries to solve: firstly how it was that one of the gates had stood across the line at the time George Hind had passed, yet later on trains had been able to pass the crossing; and, secondly, the identity of the murderer.

Jane's daughter, Elizabeth Waite, gave evidence at the inquest. She had lived with her widowed mother for nearly two years up to the Saturday before her death, when she had travelled to Liverpool to meet up with her husband, a sailor, taking her children with her. She provided details of the stolen property: three silver spoons, a gold ring and several items of jewellery. Between £6 and £7 in cash was missing, as well as 15s in silver and some gold. Of the drawers, the middle one only was locked, and it was from this the stolen property had been taken, the drawer having been forced. She identified the slasher as her mother's. It was used to break the window, as well as to strike Jane on the head at some point.

Inspector Taylor told the inquest jury he found pools of blood about eight yards from the cottage door and opposite the window. Having been directed by the Chief Constable to preserve all footprints, he covered these up with buckets and pails, and called a sculptor, Joseph Pickering, to take plaster of Paris casts. Taylor had remained at the scene during this time to ensure all the 'footsteps', about twelve in all, were preserved.

Taylor noted from the footprints that Jane's killer had stood at the south-east gatepost of the crossing, then walked along the south side of the tracks and crossed the rails to within four yards of the cottage door. At some point along this course he attacked Jane. He traced the footprints back across to the south side again, but this time they were farther apart, as though made by someone running. There were distinctive nail marks, set in a particular pattern, in the clay. He traced 'bloody footsteps' from the pool of blood near the cottage to the garden gate, then went into the garden and traced the same footprints. In the pool of blood where Jane had lain he found another footprint. Here the blood had congealed, indicating this one has been made some time after the attack.

Jane had secured the cottage door by inserting a nail into a hole by the sneck (catch). The intruder had not understood how this operated, and had kicked the door in; there was an impression of a footprint on a panel, the same as those found by the tracks. Taylor was told Jane had owned a pickaxe. It was missing from the shed, and he and others looked for it, finding it underneath the bed. There was blood on the handle. The pickaxe exactly matched marks found on the door and the drawer. Taylor also found an iron pin, over 2ft long, used to fasten back one of the gates. It was lying on the tracks and there was blood on it.

The garden gate also had a unique means of being fastened: it closed with an ordinary sneck, and a pin ran through the gatepost into the framework of the gate. A stranger would not know how to open it, especially at night. As the gate was undamaged, whoever opened it knew how to do so and also knew that the pickaxe was kept in the shed. In short, the man who murdered Jane Emmerson almost certainly knew her, and knew her duties regarding the crossing gates. He would have known that her daughter would have only recently left the cottage. He had waited by the gates in the darkness and attacked Jane.

Dr Carlyle observed of Jane Emmerson, 'I have never heard of any person having so much clothing on her head.' The first covering was a cloth-lined bonnet lined with wadding; next was a handkerchief tied over the crown; then a cap, over which was some thick flannel doubled over and tied round the head; then came a silk skull cap and over that another handkerchief. The implication was that when Jane was attacked and struck on the head, the blow failed to knock her unconscious, the impact being reduced by so much padding. She may have been struck in the first instance with the iron pin. In the opinion of both Dr Carlyle and Mr Page, the surgeon who carried out the post-mortem examination, the slasher 'would have cause the wounds' to her face and head when she was lying on the ground. The body was found 'quite warm', with no rigidity. While this might at first indicate the attack had been recent, it was pointed out that despite the ferocity of the attack and the injuries to the head, no vital organs had been pierced; hence life would have been present for some time. She was probably attacked between 9.45 p.m. and 10 p.m. on Thursday night, just after Thompson drove the last train through.

It would be thirty days after the crime before the police arrested their prime suspect. He was William Charlton, 35, a train driver who lived nearby at Harraby Street. The facts, when unravelled, would prove just how wicked and heartless he was, and what made his crime worse was that even as the police were piecing together the evidence against him, Charlton, desperate to avoid justice, contrived to put the blame on someone else, his brother-in-law, an innocent man who was arrested and held for a crime he did not commit.

On the night of the murder, James Carruthers, railway pointsman, was at his post in his cabin, between the crossing and the engine sheds. At 4 a.m. he saw Charlton approaching the cabin from the direction of the crossing – and Jane's cottage. In the years Carruthers had known Charlton he had never before seen him approach from that direction at such a time. This was hardly surprising, since Charlton was walking towards his own house. He had not spent the night elsewhere, as William Chambers had 'knocked him

An old print of Durran Hill railway crossing. (Carlisle Record Office)

up' at 3 a.m. Carruthers asked Charlton what he was doing, but did not catch Charlton's reply. Carruthers, familiar with the engine sheds, said he knew there was a 'necessary' there, meaning a toilet, so Charlton's unexpected appearance at his cabin would not have been to relieve himself.

We know that the first train to leave Carlisle that morning was the 4.20 a.m. mineral train to Newcastle. The second, another mineral train, left Carlisle at 4.30 a.m., also bound for Newcastle. The driver was Charlton, and John Mitchell was his fireman. When Charlton arrived at the engine shed, Chambers told Mitchell to oil the engine because Charlton had to return home to fetch his breakfast, which he had apparently forgotten. Thus, having arrived, Charlton left again, ostensibly to return home – but was seen not long afterwards by Carruthers approaching his cabin from the direction of the cottage.

Charlton and Mitchell left on the 4.30 a.m. train. Approaching the crossing, Charlton asked Mitchell whether the plants in a nearby field were cabbages. It was a bizarre question to say the least, considering the two men had worked together for three years, and had passed Durran Hill countless times. It was probably asked to distract Mitchell, who may otherwise have noticed that Jane's lantern was not visible. Later, at Newcastle station, the fireman on the following train from Carlisle, a man named Pigg, asked Mitchell if he 'saw a signal light' at the crossing. 'What makes you ask that?' replied Mitchell. He was told Jane's body had been discovered. Mitchell then asked Charlton if he had seen a light. 'Yes I did,' Charlton replied. 'In fact I saw the old woman in the porch.' On their return journey Mitchell remarked they probably had a tramp in custody. A likely fellow, said Charlton.

Elizabeth Waite, Jane's daughter, said Charlton knew her mother very well. He had a garden on the south side of the railway. This was corroborated by William Shepherd, a platelayer, who said Charlton had access to Jane's garden and he had seen him twice using her pick. He had also seen him inside Jane's cottage a few times.

But it was on the murderer's footwear that this case rested. The distinctive footprints found at the scene could only have belonged to one particular pair of boots or shoes. There was – or had been – a double row of sparables (nails) around the front of the soles, and 'two curved rows which formed with the sides of the boots two ellipses'. Having had plaster casts made, tracings were drawn up for comparisons with the boots of the chief suspect, William Charlton.

On 22 December, Inspectors Taylor and Douglas saw Charlton at Carlisle railway station. Charlton admitted he had arrived at the engine sheds on 21 November at about 3.20 a.m., and had told William Chambers to tell his fireman, Mitchell, to oil the engine as he was going home to get his breakfast. Inspector Taylor then walked from the engine shed to the crossing, opened the south-west gate to clear the line, went to the cottage and back to Petteril bridge point, where Carruthers had seen Charlton. It took 13 minutes. Clearly, Charlton had had time to return to the scene of the crime and see to the gates so that the trains could get through.

Taylor and Douglas then accompanied Charlton to his house in Harraby Street, where he was asked to produce his boots and shoes. He wore a pair of boots on his feet, and owned a pair of strong shoes. The latter had been newly nailed, and there were marks where two semi-circles of nails had been removed. Taylor compared these with a tracing copied from the plaster casts. They matched exactly. Asked why the nails were 'out of the shoes', Charlton said they might have been 'knocked out by the engine', or they might have been removed by Thomas Robinson, his brother-in-law. Told that the man who had worn the shoes had committed murder, Charlton said, 'I would not harm the old woman. I was not there. I know nothing about it.' His attention was drawn to what looked like blood on the shoes. 'This is not blood,' he said, 'it's grease off the engine.' Despite this claim Charlton was arrested and appeared before the magistrates the following day, charged with murder. While in custody, Charlton, knowing positive identification of the shoes meant their wearer would be identified as Jane's killer, elected to make a voluntary statement. An extract from it reads:

On 21st November I went home from work about 5.20 p.m. Afterwards I came out and went into the reading room and over to the engine sheds. When I came from there Thomas Robinson, my brother-in-law, was at the railway yard gates. We went into David Hall's public house and had a pint of ale. While in there he asked me to lend him my shoes as the roads were very clarty (muddy) and his boots were rather tight. So I lent him my shoes. They are the shoes the police showed at the Courthouse. When we came out I left him at the door. He said he was going to Ivegill. Chambers called me up the following morning, a few minutes past three o'clock. When I was coming out of the house Robinson came out of our petty (privy) and gave me my shoes back again. I asked him where he had been till this time in the morning. He said 'I have had a bloody good spree'. When I gave him my shoes in David Hall's the nails were in the shoes and I did not observe them out until Saturday night, when I was cleaning them. I have told Robinson never to come near my house again as he was such a bad 'un.

Thomas Robinson lived with Charlton and his wife in Harraby Street. The police arrested him. He denied murdering Jane and provided an alibi, saying he was miles away at Ivegill. Indeed, he had slept all night in the same bed as two other men (as they did then). His account was supported by six people, who trekked in and out of the court to rule him out of the frame.

On 31 December, Inspectors Taylor and Douglas returned to Charlton's house. They made a further search and discovered a wall that ran between an ash pit and the privy. Standing on the privy, Douglas found a hole between the top of the wall and the roof inside which was a parcel containing 52 worn sparables wrapped in paper. A pair of pincers and a chisel had earlier been found in the house. The holes in the shoes, left after the removal of the sparables, totalled 54: '13 on one side and 14 on the other' in each shoe. The game was up for William Charlton, who stood trial at Carlisle the following February. He pleaded not guilty to murder.

Edwin Price, prosecuting, said, 'The murder must have been committed by someone who knew what Jane's duties were, knew the arrangement of the trains and would take the trouble to go back and put the gates right for the first train to go through.' One by one the witnesses testified, piecing together a sequence of events damning William Charlton. A particularly sickening feature of the evidence was Charlton returning to the crossing between three and four o'clock on the morning to ensure the gates were open for the first train, when he would have stood in the congealed blood. Was it possible Jane was still alive then, slowly bleeding to death by the side of the tracks? Was this the moment he struck her with the slasher to finish her off?

Campbell Foster, defending, declared, 'A more improbable story was never hurled against a man's head.' The evidence was circumstantial. He challenged much of it, particularly the footprints, trying to cast doubt in the mind of the jury that they were made by Charlton's shoes. No blood was found on his shoes or clothing; no stolen property was found in his possession. Charlton

Plaque on the gaol wall, Carlisle. William Charlton's was the last execution in the city. (Paul Heslop)

had falsely stated his brother-in-law had borrowed his boots, not out of malice, but because he could see he would be wrongly convicted and was desperate enough to say anything. 'If you find the prisoner guilty it will send him to a doom from which he cannot escape. Better not depend on circumstances like these…'

But the jury did depend on the circumstances. They returned a guilty verdict, albeit with a recommendation to mercy on the grounds of previous good character. Charlton seemed the least concerned, possibly because he didn't hear the verdict. He was deaf, probably through years of working on a locomotive footplate. One wonders that if he didn't hear the jury's verdict, if he heard the evidence at his trial? Justice Willes put on the black cap and told Charlton not to be optimistic about receiving mercy. As he spoke, the governor of the gaol attempted to relate his words to Charlton, but 'was too much affected'. Justice Willes passed the inevitable sentence and Charlton was taken down to the cells.

THE EXECUTION

William Charlton was hanged at Carlisle Gaol at noon on 15 March 1862, in the presence of a crowd numbering between 6,000 and 8,000 people. It was the last public execution in the city. As the *Carlisle Journal* reported, 'How previous good character could afford any extenuation for so atrocious a crime, we are unable to say'. Among Charlton's visitors were his wife (who was expecting their fourth child), as well as four sisters and two brothers. Innocent men, he told them, had been hung before, and his case would add to the number.

'Zealous advocates of the abolition of capital punishment' lost no time in petitioning the Home Secretary in favour of commuting the sentence. But the minister regretted there were no grounds for advising Queen Victoria to interfere with the due course of the law. Charlton made no confession, although, paradoxically, he agreed he had had a fair trial. He did, at least, exonerate his brother-in-law: rumours persisted that Thomas Robinson was involved. In this matter Charlton was approached by the prison surgeon and asked directly if the statement made to the police, that he had lent Robinson his shoes, true or false? It was untrue, he said.

The railway company arranged free trips to Silloth to try and reduce the size of the crowd, but to no avail, as people of 'all ages, sizes and sexes' moved about in the vicinity of the gaol 'anxious to catch a glimpse of the scaffold', and scripture readers circulated leaflets, proclaiming 'Whosoever hateth his brother is a murderer'. At eleven o'clock a 'dense mass' occupied English Street, mainly men, but here and there were seen 'the bright ribbons on the bonnets of women', many carrying babes in arms. At noon the prison bell tolled and Charlton was brought to the scaffold. Standing on the platform, he cast his eyes down Botchergate for a moment. Calcraft, the hangman, reported afterwards that his very last words were that he was 'perfectly innocent of the offence'.

THE VERDICT

William Charlton was a man who had employment, as a train driver. He had a wife and children, and a better house than many others of his status: what on earth made him murder Jane Emmerson? Maybe he thought – as was rumoured – that she was a 'rich old lady' with lots of money? We will never know.

He clearly meant to rob Jane, but did he intend to kill her? Maybe his intention was to knock her unconscious, leaving him free to break into the cottage; but because she had so much clothing on her head he failed to knock her out. Did she turn and see his face in the moonlight? Did he panic and strike her in an unintended frenzied attack? We will never know that either.

There is a case for stating that Charlton did not have a fair trial: of what was said in court he heard little. In prison, he was provided with a newspaper containing a report of the trial, to read what his deafness had debarred him from hearing. After reading it 'very carefully' he said he did not see how the jury could have come to any other conclusion – yet he still maintained his innocence. He was guilty of the brutal murder of a defenceless woman, yet the jury recommended mercy. Perhaps it was to ease their own consciences, such was their awful duty. He hardly earned their recommendation, especially after alleging his brother-in-law had borrowed his shoes and thus by implication was Jane's killer.

That justice was done here was down to good coppering. Credit where it's due.

7

SUFFER THE LITTLE CHILDREN

Penrith, 1877

Isabella Carruthers, a domestic servant at the Griffin Inn, Penrith, had noticed the smell. She thought it came from a large box, one of several in the lumber-room, so she asked her employer, Mrs Jameson, if she might open it. Permission granted, she untied the cords that secured it. When she looked inside she saw 'a lot of things', including a small trunk, which was not locked or otherwise secured. She was astonished at what she found inside: a dead child, wrapped in a black skirt.

She told Mrs Jameson, who called the police. Sergeant Fraser attended. He formed the opinion the child had been dead for some years as the body was very decomposed, and took it to the police station. The following day, Friday 26 January, an inquest was held at the inn. First, the jury viewed the body, which had been brought back to the inn and placed into the box in which it was found. A juryman remarked that it might have been a monkey 'as some of that class of animal were sometimes kept there' (at the inn). This brought laughter, but such was the state of the body that the coroner directed that a medical examination should take place immediately.

Dr Thompson confirmed the body was human, but could not say if it was a boy or a girl. There was no doubt the child had been strangled, as a piece of cord had been tightly tied around its neck. Neither could he say if the child had been alive at the time of strangulation, but he thought it probable. Sergeant Fraser, who was present, told the inquest that as well as the piece of cord there was a piece of cloth over the upper part of the body and the mouth, tightly tied round the neck and knotted, and on top of that a black ribbon, tied and knotted behind the neck so tightly the doctor could not insert his finger. The jury's verdict was, simply, 'found dead'.

After the inquest, Sergeant Fraser again searched the box. He found a bundle containing wallpaper, some pieces of carpet, a blanket, a bloodstained sheet and what he thought was a woman's nightdress. The latter was wrapped around the body of a second child. This body was in an advanced state of decomposition, being dry and mummified, and had evidently been placed in the box first. It was 'dreadfully mutilated', and appeared to have been crushed by some heavy weight as one leg and a shoulder blade had been broken, and the right arm had been pressed into the right breast. Dr Thompson thought it had been in the box for about two years.

Two dead babies, the first almost certainly murdered by strangulation or suffocation. Who were they, and who was responsible for their deaths?

They were the babies of Elizabeth Kirkbride (*née* Hayton), a widow, late of Helton, near Askham, and Langwathby. It was she who arranged with William Jameson, proprietor of the Griffin Inn, the previous June, to have three boxes delivered for storage until she could pay for them to be taken to Liverpool, where she would live with her son. It was she who then had them taken to the inn. And she was the person the police needed to find and bring to justice. It didn't take long.

Just two days in fact, the time it took for the magistrates at Penrith to issue a warrant, and for Sergeant Robinson of Liverpool police to call at Mrs Kirkbride's address at 21 Sutton Street, Tuebrook. His knock was answered at 10.45 p.m. by Mrs Kirkbride. The policeman had her description, and knew he had found the right person. He told her that he had a warrant. 'What is it for?' she asked. He read it to her. She told him that she would put on her bonnet and shawl and go with him, but first she would write a note for her son who was in bed and whom she did not wish to disturb. She wrote the note and left it on a table. She then accompanied Sergeant Robinson to Old Swan police station, saying no one knew anything about the matter, which she expected to be hushed up at Penrith. It would be kept a secret at Tuebrook too, she added.

Kirkbride had taken up lodgings in Liverpool with Mrs Emma Oberti, at Sutton Street. First she took one room, then the front parlour and bedroom for her two youngest sons, John Sydney, aged 19, a grocer's assistant, and his 16-year-old brother. On the day of the arrest, Mrs Oberti went to bed at 10.15 p.m., so was unaware of the visit by the police. She came downstairs

'Horrible Discovery'. How the Carlisle Journal *reported the discovery of 'dead infants at Penrith and Liverpool'.*

THE CARLISLE JOURNAL.
FRIDAY. FEBRUARY 2. 1877.

HORRIBLE DISCOVERY

CONCEALMENT OF FIVE INFANTS.

FURTHER DISCLOSURES IN LIVERPOOL.

The discovery last week of the dead bodies of two infants at the Griffin Inn, Penrith, where they had been left last June by a widow named Kirkbride, who was schoolmistress at Langwathby, has been followed this week by the discovery of the mouldering remains of three other infants in a box in a house at Tuebrook, near Liverpool, where the woman had gone to lodge after leaving the Penrith district, seven months ago.

the following morning with Kirkbride's sons and their friend, a young man named Tyson, who shared their bedroom. They left for work, leaving her alone. When she went into the parlour she saw the fire had not been made, and thought she would ask John Sydney about it. When he did not come home for dinner, she decided to go and seek him. She met him on the way and enquired of his mother. She had gone to Penrith, he said, but would be back in a few days. Had she left any money? Mrs Oberti asked. She had not.

Mrs Oberti came to the point. The fact was, certain articles, including a coat, were missing from the house, said Mrs Oberti, meaning she believed Mrs Kirkbride had either stolen or pawned them. She had never trusted her, ever since she arrived at the house with only an umbrella to her name.

Mrs Oberti and John Sydney went to the house together, where he produced some glasses and books as security. They would not do, she said. So he went upstairs, saying, 'She has got some boxes'. So she had, tin boxes she'd had delivered after moving into the house. He wrenched the lock off one and took it from the landing into the bedroom, but came downstairs saying there was 'nothing particular in it'. He said the other box would be the same, but he had not broken it open. After he returned to work, Mrs Oberti went upstairs and with difficulty removed the tight-fitting lid of the box he had opened. When she did 'the stench was something fearful'. She closed the lid, took the box outside and sent for John Sydney, demanding he looked inside. He saw what he thought were old clothes, which he removed, then came to a piece of 'smelly substance' which Mrs Oberti thought to be 'part of a child'. She told him to go back to work and called the police.

Two constables arrived at the house and removed the contents of the box. First they unfastened the wrappings around what appeared to be a rag doll, in 'a rotten and fearful state'. It was a young, decomposed child. There was a second parcel, more rotten than the first, containing another decomposed child. This one was headless. The policemen put everything back into the box and took it away. The second box contained nothing suspicious. The next day, Tuesday 30 January, Inspector Walsh and Dr Henry Pitts went to the mortuary and examined the contents of the box: old sheets, carpets, assorted rags, and the human remains. There was a brass plate attached to the handle, with the name 'Mrs Hayton' engraved on it.

Dr Pitts examined the remains. The first child was newborn, but he could not ascertain what sex it was. It may have been in the box for up to five years. A strip of old rag was around its neck, tied in a knot, the circumference of the loop so small it must have been tied very tightly. The headless child, also newborn, was in a more advanced state of decay. It had been in the box for perhaps eight years. The remaining bones were that of the missing head – and, as Dr Pitts realised, a third child, which he estimated to have been in the box for nine or ten years. He was unable to say if any of the children had been born alive.

Five dead babies, all wrapped and stuffed into boxes at different times over the past ten years or so, two of them with ligatures around their necks. Elizabeth Kirkbride had a lot to answer for. And answer she did, but with no apparent repentance. When Inspector Walsh told her that in addition to the charge of concealing the two babies at Penrith she faced a further charge of concealing three more, she replied, 'Yes, they are all my children. I admit that I concealed them and neglected them, but I deny that I murdered any of them.'

On 1 February, a sixth dead infant was found, this time buried in the garden of the house at Helton, where Kirkbride had lived with her mother.

William Ernest Kirkbride, who had lived with his paternal grandmother, also at Helton, had been a frequent visitor to his mother's house, and five or six years before he and Alfred, his brother, had been sweeping out a loft there. As they swept towards the bottom of the steps they began to throw the dirt into a midden when William saw a white bag. It was tied up with string, which he loosened. When he looked inside he saw a red flannel petticoat, all stained, among a lot of rags. He also saw a mummified dead child. The 'little fingers and toes were quite perfect', and there was some white hair on its head. He threw it onto the midden.

William was about 13 years old at the time. He did not mention the find to his mother. Instead, he told his grandmother and two aunts. They told him to say nothing about it. He returned the next day to dig in the garden, and noticed some flock on the ground, partly covered with earth. He knocked it aside with his spade and discovered the same dead child. It had been buried with 'just a little earth spread over it'. He threw some earth over the body and did not visit the site again until 1877 when, accompanied by PC Reed, he indicated the spot where he had found the child. Charged with concealing this birth, Kirkbride made no reply.

Elizabeth Mary Louise Kirkbride was 41 years old. Her parents were respectable people who had lived in Liverpool, where she was born. She was their only daughter, and 'great pains had been bestowed' on her education. Evidently she could speak several languages. She married young, and when her husband died in 1864, her income died with him, so she went to live with her mother at Helton. Her conduct at that time was described as 'restless' and 'eccentric'; she would be seen at all hours of the night, wandering the country lanes where 'nothing annoyed her more than having the light from the local policeman's lantern thrown upon her face'.

She had four sons, two of whom lived at Tuebrook. Two others, William Ernest, now 18, and Alfred, had lived with their paternal grandmother, Margaret Kirkbride, at Helton. Mrs Kirkbride was a teacher. In 1876, she and her mother moved to Langwathby, where she took up a position at a school. This did not last long, as there was only one pupil. Times were hard. First, her mother died. Then she fell into debt and her goods were seized or sold off. So she went to live in Liverpool, at the address of Mrs Oberti. In the course

Helton, 2007. (Paul Heslop)

of moving she deposited the boxes at the Griffin Inn. But not all of them. Others were deposited at the left luggage office at Aintree railway station, Liverpool, where they remained until 29 July, when she had them taken to 21 Sutton Street. Before they were brought to her, observed Mrs Oberti, she 'never rested in the house'; she was in and out continually and couldn't seem to settle. When the boxes came she took them upstairs, spurning Mrs Oberti's offer to help, saying she could manage herself.

On 8 February, after her arrest, Inspector Walsh received a message that Kirkbride wanted to see him. He went to her cell, where she made a verbal statement, saying, 'I want to tell you who the father is of all the children I am here about. His name is Thomas Moss. He is a tea, ham and bacon dealer in Askham, near Penrith. He is the only man I have ever had anything to do with, and I think it only right he should be exposed as it is entirely by his own persuasion that I am placed as I am, and he had always promised that he will make me his wife. Instead of doing so, when he was in a position he married another.'

There seems little doubt that all six dead infants were born at Helton, and disposed of, or 'concealed' there, by their mother, one being buried, and the remainder put into boxes. There can be little doubt, too, that the father was Thomas Moss, who was having a relationship with Kirkbride and who, according to her statement, had promised to marry her. Going to and from to his house at Askham she had been seen by the local policeman, 'wandering the country lanes', loth to be seen abroad. It would not do to be having illegitimate children, which she could not support. She had been widowed;

times were hard; she needed a man to provide and she had found one, or so she thought.

Moss was never arrested. This seems strange; after all, he must have known of her repeated pregnancies and perhaps dreaded the possibility of having children to maintain. Surely the police should at least have questioned him. Instead, he remained untouched by the not so long arm of the law. Neither did he step forward to speak on behalf of the woman who had borne him six children, and whom he had evidently promised to marry. He lacked any trace of decency or moral fibre.

There was a problem in choosing the venue of Kirkbride's trial. Two of the children had been found at Penrith, in Cumberland, three had been found in Liverpool and the sixth had been found buried at Helton, in Westmorland. It was decided that her trial would be in the latter county, where she had given birth to them all. It took place at the Shire Hall, Appleby on 23 February 1877. Described as 'a widow, of superior education', she pleaded guilty to unlawfully attempting to conceal the birth of three of her children. But why only three? The answer is because the authorities would not allow any more charges. She could not be charged with murder, as it could not be proved any had been born alive. Even so, dreadful punishment would surely follow.

Justice Manisty told Kirkbride, 'You have acted as a mother so inhuman that the case is almost without a parallel. It has been a matter of concern as to whether you should have been tried for murder. I am bound to say that you have been guilty of violence towards your children when they were alive. I cannot discover any reason why cord was tied around the necks of those children, deep enough and tight enough to cause death. In another of the cases there are marks of fearful violence – the head severed from the body of the child. I am going to pass a severe sentence: nine months' imprisonment in the case of each of the three indictments – in aggregate two years and three months with hard labour.' Kirkbride, who reportedly 'maintained a demeanour of the greatest composure', was then removed. An educated lady who spoke several languages, she may yet have succeeded, after her release, in carving out a decent living, or found the husband she wanted. Who knows?

THE VERDICT

If ever a woman had a right to feel bitter at the way she was treated by a man it was Elizabeth Kirkbride. She wanted a husband; Thomas Moss falsely promised it would be him. And so he had his wicked way while she gave birth to at least six unwanted children. Although none was proven to have been born alive, it surely cannot be that all six died naturally. Two had ligatures around their necks – why, if not to kill? A sentence of twenty-seven months' imprisonment was risible.

Or was it? Elizabeth Kirkbride fell on hard times when her husband died. After his death she needed help, more so when her endeavours to earn an

The Shire Hall, Appleby. (Paul Heslop)

income by teaching failed. She had no income and no pension. With no birth control either, she repeatedly fell pregnant, always in the hope that Thomas Moss would, as he promised, be her breadwinner. Six babies born, six lives taken. But the judge was quite wrong in saying, 'You have been guilty of violence towards your children when they were alive,' as there was no proof that she was. She was charged with concealment, not murder. Twenty-seven months, in the circumstances, might not have been so lenient.

Why did she pack five of her babies into boxes and keep their little bodies? Was it a gesture to ease her conscience? Was she trying to hang on to something she loved but could not have? If she was party to their deaths, she may have thought she was helping them by taking them from a world in which she could not provide. Or maybe she was acting under the coercion of others, agreeing, however reluctantly, that it was better that way. But who, if not she, killed her children? Thomas Moss would not have wanted babies. Was it he who tied the ligatures, who perhaps suffocated the others? There was reason to enquire, surely. Yet Moss, it seems, avoided investigation. So, for that matter, did Kirkbride's mother-in-law, who told her grandson to say nothing when told he had found a child buried in the garden. Elizabeth Kirkbride may not have been alone in this catalogue of crime, but she alone faced the consequences.

8

A CAMPAIGN OF CRIME

Carlisle, Plumpton, Tebay, 1885

Responding to a report of a burglary at Netherby Hall, near Longtown, Sergeant John Roche and PC Jacob Johnstone could not have foreseen the events that were to occur when they stopped four suspects at Kingstown, near Carlisle, after 10 p.m. on a moonlit October night. Asked where they had come from and where they were going, one of the men replied, 'What business is that of yours?' Sergeant Roche told him they were police officers. 'I'll give you police officer,' said the man, drawing a billhook from his coat pocket and aiming a blow at the policeman's head. Roche drew his staff and struck the man – only to see two of the man's companions pointing revolvers at him.

Roche was shot in the arm, and struck several blows to the back of the neck and head. As PC Johnstone went to his assistance, Roche got to his feet and together they ran after the men. After some 25 yards, PC Johnstone reached out to grab one of the men, when another turned and shot him in the chest. The men escaped into the darkness. Their escape south along the railway included a vicious assault on another policeman, the fatal shooting of a third and, ultimately, their apprehension – not by law officers but by railway workers.

The story of the Netherby burglars is etched into Cumbrian history. It has all the ingredients to satisfy the requirements of a movie: courage and determination in the face of violence and, not least, drama. From the encounter with the two policemen at Kingstown, the men were tracked through Carlisle and southwards to Plumpton, before continuing – by train – to Tebay in Westmorland, where two were apprehended, and the third at Lancaster.

They were three in number: Anthony Benjamin Rudge, aged 45, John Martin (alias John White), aged 36, and James Baker, aged 29. All had 'form' and had served sentences of penal servitude. The fourth man was not, it seems, a member of the gang, although there may be room to question this supposition. It seems Rudge and Martin left London together and met up with Baker at Manchester, whence they went to Northumberland and then on to Liverpool on a campaign of burglaries. On Tuesday 27 October 1885,

The Graham Arms, Longtown. (Paul Heslop)

having arrived at Longtown via Gretna, they learned by chance of a baronet who lived at nearby Netherby Hall. Paying him a surprise visit would have been too good an opportunity to pass up.

Rudge, Martin and Baker were spotted by Alexander Maclean, stationmaster at Gretna, when they arrived on the 9.10 a.m. train. They carried three portmanteaus (large travel bags), which Maclean agreed to put into his office. They were seen again that evening at the Bush Hotel, Longtown, where they had dinner. At 11.20 a.m. the following morning they were seen by Mary Richardson at Netherby, wearing long, dark overcoats and distinctive hats. Rudge asked her if the master of 'the big house' was at home. She told him all the family were, whereupon he enquired of the name of the owner. 'Sir Frederick Graham,' she told him. Later, Rudge asked William Atkinson, a carter, if Sir Frederick was at home. 'He was when I came away,' Atkinson replied.

Later that day one of the gang returned to Gretna and collected one of the portmanteaus, which he took to the Graham Arms Hotel, Longtown. David Johnstone, the landlady's son-in-law, observed the three in the hotel. The portmanteau was taken back to the station, where Baker took some 'articles of apparel' from it, before locking it again and telling the stationmaster, Maclean, they would require a cab for Longtown. They would have to walk, he was told. 'In that case,' said Baker, 'you may as well forward them (the portmanteaus) to Carlisle.' 'In what name?' Maclean asked. 'Oh, A. Smith,' said Baker. The portmanteaus were labelled accordingly and sent to Carlisle.

The protagonists anticipated correctly that dinner at Netherby Hall would be taken at about 8 p.m. When a housemaid, Annie Carnew, had occasion

Netherby Hall as it was. (Carlisle Record Office)

to visit the master bedroom at that hour she found nothing unusual and left the door unlocked on her departure. At 8.15 p.m. the door was found locked and the alarm was raised. Joseph Plenderleith, a valet, wasted no time. He ran outside, got a ladder and climbed up to the open window. His promptness was commendable, but he was too late. The lid of a dressing case had been broken open, and jewels to the value of £250 had been stolen. The following morning Plenderleith found another ladder. This one was shorter and had been placed on a bench to enable the intruders to climb through the window.

Information was quickly passed to the police at Carlisle, and from there 'means were taken to raise the whole county'. The police would be watching the roads. At Kingstown, PC Johnstone had gone to bed, only to be woken by Sergeant Roche. When Roche stepped onto the road, he saw four men approaching from Longtown and called for Johnstone to join him. He did so in shirtsleeve order and no helmet. Rudge, Martin and Baker wore their dark overcoats; the fourth man, wearing a light overcoat, would never be identified or apprehended. Despite facing men with guns, both officers nevertheless attempted to arrest them, and were shot in the process.

Half a mile south, PC Handley had heard the shots. As a result he called upon two neighbours, Mr Armstrong and Mr Hetherington, for assistance. This was about 11.15 p.m. Both men left their houses to assist the constable. Sure enough, they encountered four men on the road. One of them said, 'We have been assaulted by two men back there.' 'I will have to detain you until I have seen about that assault,' replied PC Handley. He took hold of the man, who put a pistol to the constable's chest. Another of the men brandished a pistol at Armstrong, who held up his lamp. 'Leave go, Handley, and let's be out of this,' declared Armstrong. The four men then made off towards Carlisle. Discretion was the better part of valour on this occasion. They had nevertheless challenged the men, even when knowing shots had been fired.

The men didn't proceed into the centre of Carlisle. Instead, they crossed the River Eden by the old North British railway bridge and followed the line towards the southern part of the city. At 2.30 a.m. on Thursday morning they were spotted passing the signal box on the Dalston road. PC Fortune was waiting for them. 'Hallo chaps. What's up here at this time of the morning?' he asked. The reply was a blow to the left side of his head, which knocked him unconscious. When he awoke he found himself at the bottom of the embankment and the men had gone. He had been attacked with a jemmy, beaten and left unconscious, with nineteen wounds to the head.

Fortune clambered up the embankment, where he was spotted by the signalman, Thomas Evans, who described his condition as 'dreadful'. Evans cleaned his face up, gave him something to eat, and then helped him to the street. Fortune was lucky to survive. In a post-conviction statement, Baker said Rudge and Martin placed the unfortunate constable over the rails so that when a train went over him it would appear to be an accident. But he, Baker, went back and threw him down the embankment.

Throughout that day, it is believed the men hid in the woods near Wreay. Then the fourth man went his own way, and Rudge, Martin and Baker continued south along the railway. At 5 p.m. the stationmaster at Calthwaite, John Hayes, was visited by PC Joseph Byrnes, of Plumpton, who told him about the burglary and the attacks on Roche, Johnstone and Fortune. The constable said it would be 'rash to attack the men', whom he knew to be armed. Just after 7 p.m. Hayes saw the three enter the station waiting room. Rudge enquired about a train to Penrith, but the last train had gone. Hayes sent a telegram to Plumpton, two and a half miles down the line. As a result William Lowthian, who was in Plumpton station, went for PC Byrnes. Meanwhile, at about 8.20 p.m., Thomas Simpson encountered Robert Nicholson near the vicarage gate. As they chatted, three men passed by, in the direction of the Pack Horse Inn. When Simpson and Nicholson parted, the former encountered PC Byrnes walking towards the Pack Horse. He was wearing a plain topcoat over his uniform and a slouch hat. The constable hurried towards the inn.

In the Pack Horse, Ann Griffiths, the licensee, had seen two strangers enter the bar at about 8.35 p.m. One, later identified as Baker, had an overcoat on; the other, possibly Rudge, did not. The men asked for two gills of beer and some bread and cheese. They drank the beer, and two more gills besides, and took the food away with them along with a pint bottle of rum. They were in the pub for about five minutes. They said they had a long drive, and were tired and hungry.

PC Joseph Byrne was a native of County Down, Northern Ireland. He came to England to seek employment and worked as a miner in the Millom area before enlisting with the Cumbria Constabulary, where he served at Harrington, Alston and Plumpton. He was a married man, aged 34, with four children, when he was murdered.

Joseph Byrne was interred at Penrith cemetery on 1 November 1885. An estimated 3,000 people attended. Addressing those present, the Revd Father Meynell said, 'Unarmed, he had nevertheless gone to confront men whom he knew were armed and had already used arms against the police...' The Chief Constable sent a letter to the murdered officer's widow, expressing his 'deep sympathy' and sent £30 'to defray all expenses of his funeral', which was attended by a superintendent and a detachment of constables but not, sadly, himself. (Courtesy of Mr Brian Parnaby)

Shortly afterwards, Elizabeth Irving, housemaid at the vicarage, and her daughter, Margaret, heard a shot. Nothing more is recorded until Thomas Lowthian left the Pack Horse at about 10 p.m. and walked towards the station. On the road, near the vicarage, he heard the sound of moaning. He looked over a stone wall, but could see nothing in the darkness. He returned to the inn for assistance. PC Byrnes was then discovered lying in the field on the opposite side of the wall. There was blood where he lay, and on the road nearby. He was carried to the Pack Horse. A medical student, William Matthew, attended the inn about midnight, finding Byrnes still alive but unconscious. He found a bullet wound 'in the left orbit' (eyeball socket). The bullet had passed through the brain and emerged half an inch behind the left ear. Byrnes died about three quarters of an hour later. Tristram Montgomery, a Penrith surgeon, carried out a post-mortem examination. He said that PC Byrnes was shot 'from the front' and the solitary bullet killed him. It was a pistol bullet wound. There was some conjecture as to the cause of marks on the officer's wrists: he may have been held as he was shot, or he may have been dragged along the road after being shot. Either way, he had been thrown over the wall and left in the field where he was found.

Three men, at least two of them armed, had been on the run for over twenty-four hours. In their wake they had left three policemen injured and another dead. The officers who had challenged them were brave and had acted beyond the call of duty, and yet these dangerous men were still free, and in days of poor communication and transport would take some capturing.

Christopher Gaddes, a goods guard on the railway.
(Courtesy of Mr Brian Parnaby)

Constable Patterson was the next policeman to play a part, when he saw three men walking in single file along the railway north of Penrith. They passed within fourteen yards of him just after 10 a.m. the following morning. He reported this to his superintendent, and then went to Penrith station where he told Christopher Gaddes, a guard on a southward-bound goods train, about the wanted men, informing him that one or more was armed. Gaddes's 'coolness and presence of mind' led ultimately to their capture.

Gaddes was a Longtown man who, ironically, had once been employed as a carter by Sir Frederick Graham at Netherby Hall. He was 24 years old and recently married. His train had been searched at Penrith, before continuing to Keswick Junction, where the former railway led off to Cockermouth. As his train pulled away, Gaddes saw three men get into a wagon. As the train passed through Shap he threw a written message from the moving train, urging the stationmaster to telegraph Tebay for assistance when the train reached that station. The message was not spotted. At Shap summit, the brakesman threw out another message. It was picked up by the driver of a stationary goods train, who then telegraphed Tebay. Railway workers, not policemen, would form the reception committee for the three desperadoes.

At Tebay station, the men bolted. George Beaty, a foreman, knocked one of them down with a brake stick. It was John Martin, who was in possession of a revolver. Robert Wills, an engine driver, shone a lantern on Anthony Rudge, who had his hand in his pocket – possibly ready to draw his revolver. Wills then hit him with a jack-bar. Rudge was seized under the bridge over the River Lune. The following morning John Wilson went to the river where he found an item of jewellery, the property of Lady Graham, and a key. The

How the Illustrated Police News *reported the crime.*

key fitted one of the portmanteaus the men had deposited at Gretna. PC Scott was told to search the river south of Tebay bridge. He was nothing if not persistent: seven days later, the river having subsided after floods, he found a tobacco pouch containing the rest of Lady Graham's jewellery.

Baker escaped capture at Tebay station. A goods train, pulling 35 wagons, left Tebay station just after midnight. The driver was Thomas Matley. As his train pulled away, Matley noticed a man spring on to a wagon. He wrote a message, which he threw from the train at Grayrigg, telling the pointsman there to wire Oxenholme that 'the burglar was on the train'. At Oxenhome three policemen searched the train but found no one. Pulling away again, Matley saw a man emerge from a hedge and get into a wagon. At Carnforth he got out and saw the man. He went for the guard, but the man disappeared. Then, as he pulled away again, he saw the same man jump into another wagon. Just before Lancaster, Matley stopped his train and saw the man peering out from under a sheet. He went to the pointsman's box and passed a message: the man was approaching the station on foot. The man, of course, was Baker.

Henry Cooper, a passenger guard, saw Matley's train arrive at Lancaster at 2.24 a.m. He was standing on the platform when Baker asked him, 'Is this the train for Crewe way?' Did he have a ticket, asked Cooper? He did not. Cooper asked him where he had come from. 'Down the goods yard, past the policeman,' said Baker. Cooper grabbed him. Baker tried to get away, but was seized by a policeman and another railway employee. The infamous trio were all captured. Baker was fortunate to stand trial at all – when he was taken to Carlisle railway station a crowd was waiting and police had to use batons to prevent him being lynched.

Meanwhile, Superintendent Sempill examined the three portmanteaus. They contained housebreaking implements, including a jemmy and chisel, ammunition and clothing. All three men stood trial at the Carlisle Assizes the following January for the murder of Byrnes. They pleaded not guilty. Mr Littler, prosecuting, said there was a singular chain of events connecting them with the crime: 'It did not matter at whose hand the particular shot was fired. They were all of reckless, uncontrollable and ferocious disposition, prepared to do anything for the purpose of escaping.'

For Rudge and Martin, Mr Cavanagh said when they 'had put their hands to their pockets where the revolvers were (on being detained) it was probable they were attempting to get hold of them for the purpose of throwing them away, thus getting rid of evidence'. The murder, he said, was committed by one person, and gave detailed reasons why this must have been Baker. But Mr Mattinson, for Baker, said at no time was it firmly established that Baker had possessed a revolver. Between them they were casting doubt as to who actually shot PC Byrnes. Doubt is all that is needed to secure acquittal, for a case must be proven 'beyond reasonable doubt'.

Mr Mattinson continued: 'Was it a murder committed by one or three persons?' There was a suggestion, he said, that two men had held PC Byrnes while a third shot him. The marks on the officer's wrists suggested this to be the case. But the marks were also consistent with being dragged after death. PC Byrnes, though brave, was a prudent man, and it would have been the height of imprudence for him to challenge three men knowing them to be armed. He might have encountered only one man on the road, and attempted to seize him. If he had encountered three, they would not have resorted to such a desperate measure.

The judge said that if the evidence satisfied the jury that PC Byrnes was shot by any one of the prisoners, 'the act of one was the act of all.' The jury agreed. Asked if they had anything to say before sentence was passed, all three had much to say – too long to include in these pages, except that Rudge at one point said, 'I confess to the murder myself but you cannot prove it. Martin and Baker are equally innocent.' He then contradicted himself by saying that they were all elsewhere, and that witnesses had lied. 'In passing death upon me,' Rudge told the court, 'you are passing the sentence that I absolutely want. I prefer it to going to the living death of penal servitude.'

The judge, 'tremulous with emotion', addressed the three men: 'I implore all of you to cast away hope in this world. Buoy not yourselves up with expectation of forgiveness. There is no hope of pardon.' After sentencing them to death, he praised the police, notably Superintendent Sempill 'in devising the admirable measures taken by him to secure the arrest of the prisoners, and the great skill, ability and judgement he displayed'; and 'the heroic conduct of Roche, Johnstone, and Fortune, and PC Byrnes, who appears to have acted as a most brave and valiant man, an admirable officer, who, knowing what he did of these men, did not hesitate to seek to arrest them'. He was also 'much pleased' at the way the railway workers acted.

For their bravery and determination, Roche and Johnstone were promoted, but PC Fortune never recovered from his injuries and retired on medical grounds. Byrnes, a Roman Catholic, was buried in Penrith cemetery in an unmarked grave. A memorial tablet can be seen, set in the stone wall at Plumpton where he was murdered, inscribed thus: 'Here Constable Joseph Byrnes fell on the night of October 29 1855, shot by the three Netherby burglars whom he, single handed, endeavoured to arrest'. Despite these words, no posthumous award was ever made to honour his bravery.

THE EXECUTIONS

The execution of Rudge, Martin and Baker was set for 8 February 1886 at Carlisle Gaol. A new gallows had been erected above a pit over 10ft deep. No longer would the

Headstone marking the grave of PC Byrnes, erected in 2006 after his resting place was traced by his great nephew, Brian Parnaby. (Paul Heslop)

waiting crowd be able to witness the event; instead, the hoisting of a black flag would signal that the due course of the law had been administered. Of the sentence, Rudge said, 'I say it is judicial murder.' Awaiting death, he spent his time writing an account of his life and the crime for which he would hang. He was unquestionably the leader of the gang. He and Martin spoke with contempt of Baker, whom they regarded as 'below them as an artist in crime'. Baker came from a respectable family, who employed a solicitor to try and have his sentence commuted. He never carried a gun and probably didn't shoot PC Byrnes, but his appeal was turned down.

Just before 8 a.m. on the day of reckoning, the three were taken from their cells. The executioner was Berry, 'a comely-looking man about 35 years of age'. Baker was 'dazed'; Martin was 'perfectly collected', the calmest of them all. Rudge, last to be taken out, stepped forward and shook hands with his fellow prisoners, saying, 'Goodbye old pal.' They formed a procession; the Protestant Baker first, Roman Catholics Rudge and Martin behind. They walked together to the drop where their names were written in chalk, indicating where each was to stand. Rudge and Martin, encouraged by their spiritual advisers, cried out, 'Lord Jesus, receive my soul.' Baker: 'Lord Jesus, have mercy upon me. I die innocent.' And, in a reference to his sweetheart, 'Nellie, keep straight.'

Berry strapped their legs, attached the noose and secured the white caps over each man's head. Signalling the men of God to stand clear, he stepped back and pulled the lever. Just as three men had committed crimes together, so they died together. Outside, a crowd of over 3,000 witnessed the raising of the black flag. Two of the gang had made last requests: Rudge, for his head to be opened after he was executed, as he believed there was 'something peculiar' about his brain (it was not carried out); and Martin, who wished it to be known that it was he who shot PC Byrnes – not to kill him, he said, but for the others to escape.

THE VERDICT

In such a campaign of crime by three men, one would have thought the question of identification would have been paramount. Yet identification hardly mattered: all three were together, and acted together, on the burglary, as well as when Sergeant Roche and PC Johnstone were shot and when PC Fortune was beaten and left for dead. But were they together when PC Byrnes was murdered?

Two of them were in the Pack Horse Inn just before the crime. Expecting to see three men, PC Byrnes may have encountered only one. The post-conviction confession of Martin seems to hold credence. He admitted to Canon Waterton that he shot PC Byrnes, and told the prison governor the 'world should be informed'. With death imminent, he had nothing to gain by lying. If so, should Martin alone have faced a murder charge? How could the others be guilty of a crime if they didn't know anything about it? It seems they could be, for they acted with continuing 'common purpose'. In any case, if their confessions are to be believed, all were present. Awaiting trial, Baker told a fellow prisoner: 'The policeman insisted on taking one of them and they fired and shot him through the head.'

The murder of PC Byrnes was a heinous crime, but we should not lose sight of the shooting of Sergeant Roche and PC Johnstone, or of the dreadful injuries suffered by PC Fortune. They were all brave men, doing their duty, namely to arrest armed criminals while they were unarmed. These were the days when policemen patrolled on foot, usually alone and without radio communication. They had to use their initiative, without recourse to backup. The citizens of Carlisle, Cumberland and Westmorland, whom they served then, can be proud of such men. Their railwaymen, too, stout fellows who, knowing armed criminals were arriving on trains, picked up what weapons they could lay their hands on and arrested them all.

If any good can be said of any of the so-called Netherby burglars, James Baker alone may have claim to mitigation. He it was who went back to the battered body of PC Fortune and rolled him down the embankment, thus saving his life. Baker did not carry a firearm; he did not shoot anyone and so felt aggrieved when, on the scaffold, he called out, 'I die innocent.' He was not innocent. None of them was.

9
A DEFECT OF REASON

Haverigg, 1892

It was 10.30 a.m. on New Year's day, and 20-year-old James Crossman was asleep on the settle in the kitchen at his parents' house at 4 Moor Moss, Haverigg. Opening his eyes sleepily, he saw Joseph Wilson, the lodger, standing in front of him, a sight that would not normally have surprised him in the slightest, except that Wilson was holding his father's double-barrelled shotgun. Still, it was not so unusual for Wilson to have the gun. He'd seen him with it before. Crossman drifted back to sleep, but suddenly the sound of a shot followed by a heavy thud awoke him from his slumber.

Seconds later, 8-year-old Richard Crossman, James's half-brother, was at the door of a neighbour, Mary Ann Johns, at 2 Moor Moss. Young Richard was crying and bleeding from the face. Whatever was the matter? Mrs Johns asked. 'Joe has done it to me and he has done it to ma too,' said Richard. Mrs Johns called upstairs to her husband, who had just gone to bed having been at work all night. Just then James Crossman, arriving in haste from his disturbed sleep on the settle, ran directly upstairs, telling Mr Johns that 'Joe had just shot his stepmother', and imploring him to go and take the gun away from him as he was afraid he would shoot him too.

Apparently ignoring any possible threat to his own safety, James Johns went to the Crossmans' house, where he saw the lifeless body of 30-year-old Marion Greaves Crossman lying face down in the doorway. Looking inside, he saw the shotgun lying against the cupboard in the front parlour. Stepping over Mrs Crossman, he picked up the gun and took it to his own house. On the way he encountered Joseph Wilson, who asked him what he was doing with the gun. Mr Johns told him, and when he examined the gun he found the left-hand barrel was loaded with a cartridge, with the trigger at half cock, and the right-hand barrel contained a cartridge that had been discharged.

Marion Crossman was the second wife of Richard Crossman, aged 41, a miner. They lived together at 4 Moor Moss, but that morning Mr Crossman had left the house at ten minutes past eight to visit his daughter by his first marriage, Mary Ann, who lived at Dalton-in-Furness. Remaining in the house that morning were James, one of his sons by his first marriage, and at least four small children from his second marriage – John, Richard junior, Frank, and 2-year-old George Alfred, as well as his wife, Marion, and Joseph Wilson,

An impression of the Crossmans' house.
(Carlisle Journal)

who had lodged with the family at that address for two months, but whom the Crossmans had known for four years.

John, aged 10, had got up at about 9 a.m. and gone downstairs to the kitchen, where he found Wilson by the fire, playing with baby George. His half-brother James was asleep on the settle. His mother was getting Wilson's breakfast. At some point she went into the front room, followed by Wilson, who took the shotgun from the kitchen mantelpiece. A quarrel ensued, during which John heard Wilson say he would 'shoot her and shoot himself'.

John went into the front room where his mother calmly said to him, 'Go for Mr Currie,' meaning the village constable. She gave him a can and a shilling, telling him to fetch a glass of ale for her. As he left the house by the front door, close to where his mother was standing, he heard a gunshot and heard his mother fall. He went back and saw his mother lying in the doorway. He then watched Wilson lift his younger brother, Frank, from where he was sitting by the fire, step over his mother and stand him up against the wall at the front of the house. John went directly to Mrs Cole's, next door, and said, 'Joseph Wilson's shot ma.' He pointed to the doorway of his house, and then ran to fetch PC Currie.

Mrs Cole went outside and saw Mrs Crossman lying just inside the doorway, face down with her feet over the doorstep. Inside the house, Joseph Wilson was standing in the doorway between the front room and the kitchen, near to the foot of the stairs. From outside, Mrs Cole asked him, 'Oh dear, whatever made you do it?' Wilson replied, 'I might as well do it as be done myself.' When she stepped forward to look closely at Marion, Wilson said, 'The first bugger that enters here I will blow their bloody brains out.' Mrs Cole screamed, which brought the neighbours out. She went into a neighbour's house and waited for PC Currie to arrive.

Eight-year-old Richard had also been in the kitchen. He too saw Wilson take the gun from the mantelpiece, and saw him load it. He was standing by the parlour door when Wilson pointed the gun at his mother. Wilson was standing by the stairs and Mrs Crossman near the front door. He would have seen Wilson shoot his mother, although he was too frightened to say so when questioned. He saw his mother fall. Some of the pellets struck him on the head, and he was in an injured state when he went to Mrs Johns' house. Wilson followed him directly to the Johns' house. Mrs Johns was frightened, and in tears she asked

The Harbour Hotel, Haverigg; scene of the first inquest into the death of Marion Crossman. (Paul Heslop)

him what he had done. He said something like, 'I know what I have done,' and to young Richard, who was also crying, he said, 'Never mind, I did not mean to hurt you.' The doctor later removed the pellets in Richard's head.

When Dr Dunn attended the scene he had no hesitation in declaring the gunshot had killed Marion Crossman. 'I came to the conclusion,' he told the inquest jury at the Harbour Hotel, Haverigg, 'that the gun must have been discharged close to the deceased, from the destruction of the bones of her skull. The distance would be about three or four yards.' The shot had 'gone in a compact body and had not had room to spread, and had a similar effect to that of a bullet'. His conclusion was that the gun was pointed at the right eye because he could find no trace of it. There were marks of shot and brain and blood on the door, and brain substance on the outside wall. 'I found some brains in the field,' he said, referring to the field immediately opposite the front door, 'and a portion of the skull some distance away.'

Richard Crossman owned the breech-loading double-barrelled shotgun, which he used to shoot wild birds and pigeons. He had last used it on 26 December. When he left the house on New Year's morning the gun was in its usual place – in the left-hand corner of his bedroom, by the window. It was not loaded, although there was ammunition to hand; four cartridges, which were kept in a tin box in the bedroom. Giving evidence at the inquests and subsequent trial, he was adamant these facts were correct. When he returned home, at 3.10 p.m. the same day, his wife was lying dead on the settle. He went upstairs but could not find the gun. As to Wilson shooting his wife, Crossman said, 'If all the people of Millom had tried to persuade me he would do it, they could not have done so.' In the years he had known Wilson, Crossman said his family, including his wife, had been on 'intimate and friendly terms with him'. He had never seen a 'quieter young man in the house than Joe'. So why would he kill Marion Crossman?

As Crossman told the court, Joseph Wilson had previously been engaged to his daughter; Mary Ann. Wilson had bought furniture, which was still in the house. But Mary Ann had run off with another young man, and now worked in service. Crossman said Wilson 'took it to heart' but nevertheless remained with the Crossman's as their lodger – and friend.

Wilson may not have had an obvious motive to shoot Marion Crossman, but there appears to have been some issue between them earlier on New Year's morning. About 8.30 a.m. Mrs Crossman called at Jane Cole's house, at 3 Moor Moss. Mrs Crossman told Mrs Cole that if Joe called she was to say she wasn't there. Wilson did call, whereupon Mrs Cole duly told him that Marion was not in. Mrs Cole then went to the Johns' house where she saw Wilson, who had called to wish Mrs Johns a happy New Year. She asked him, as was the custom, if he would like a drink. He said he would, and she gave him a glass of beer. He appeared sober and she noticed nothing unusual about him.

Mrs Cole then returned to her house, and Wilson followed. Mrs Crossman, who was still there, hid in the coalhouse. Wilson saw her and said, 'You can come out. I know you are here.' She came out and they smiled at one another. Mrs Cole, Mrs Jones and Mrs Crossman then had a drink of rum, as did Wilson when he asked for some – a small wineglassful, with water. He then asked Mrs Crossman to go and make his breakfast, and she and Mrs Jones left the house at the same time. Wilson remained with Mrs Cole, who told him to go and get his breakfast because she had work to do. To this he replied, 'Someone else will have their breakfast in another two hours.' At about 10.30 a.m., two hours later in fact, Mrs Cole heard the shot.

Mrs Cole went to her front door to see what had happened. There she encountered 10-year-old John Crossman, and then went to the Crossmans' house where she found Marion Crossman lying in the doorway and Wilson in the front room, at the foot of the stairs, the shotgun close by. As she covered Mrs Crossman's face, she saw that Wilson was smiling.

PC Currie lived in the police house at Haverigg. In days when policemen lived and worked in the same community, young John Crossman had had no difficulty in seeking him out. After sending the boy for the doctor, PC Currie hastened to the scene. Without regard for his own safety he went directly to 4 Moor Moss, where he saw Marion Crossman still lying in the doorway. He turned her lifeless body over and saw that 'the right side of her face had completely gone', and that she lay in a large pool of blood. He apprehended Joseph Wilson at once. 'You need not be in such a hurry,' said Wilson. 'I am not going to run away. I have bloody well done it. I was not sure I had done it. I put another cartridge into the gun to make bloody well sure of her.' One of the 'little children' in the house, 5-year-old Frank Crossman, was sitting on the table in his nightshirt, 'grasping the table and paralysed with fright'.

On the way to the police station, in company with Inspector Watson, Wilson had more to say. 'I made a bloody good job for the first shot and I will likely get my neck stretched too.' Watson had known Wilson for several years, and would say that his demeanour was no different to what it always

Plan of the Crossmans' house.
(Whitehaven News)

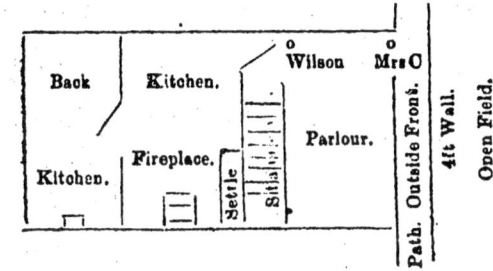

was: that he, Wilson, kept smiling. The *Whitehaven News* described him as a 'little fellow, whose face might lead to the mistaken idea that he was a mere boy of sixteen or seventeen, who appears to carry an habitual smile'.

The inquest jury's verdict was 'murder'. When he appeared before the magistrates he 'bore himself as if indifferent to the serious character of the charge against him'. He appeared at the Carlisle Assizes the following March and pleaded not guilty to murder. That he had shot Marion Crossman in cold blood was not in doubt; what was in question was his state of mind. In an act so out of character, was he not insane at the time he did it? Defence barrister, Mr Henry, was out to convince the jury that he was.

> *Mr Henry (to Dr Dunn)*: 'You noticed the condition of the prisoner at the time. What was he doing?'
> *Dr Dunn*: 'He was smiling.'
> *Mr Henry*: 'Did it strike you as unusual?'
> *Dr Dunn*: 'Yes, it did.'
> *Mr Henry*: 'Assuming he was on friendly terms with the family, did his conduct not indicate that he was not of sound mind?'
> *Dr Dunn*: 'He was not acting as a sane man would act.'

Mr Henry suggested that no sane man would have done what Joseph Wilson did. He must have completely lost his senses. A few minutes before the crime everything was amicable; then this man – this boy – takes up a gun and shoots his most intimate friend. It was temporary insanity, he claimed, without malice aforethought. He had been smiling after the deed, hardly the actions of a sane person. Dr Dunn did not think he was a man who was 'right mentally'. But Dr Dunn, far from being confined to his opinions concerning Mrs Crossman's death, found himself caught up in a ridiculous argument between Mr Henry, who sought to prove a deficiency in Wilson's intellect, and the learned judge, concerning the apparent fact that Wilson had an incomplete palate:

> *His Lordship*: 'A man may have an incomplete palate and yet have a remarkably good brain. Is that not so?'
> *Dr Dunn*: 'It may be.'

Mr Henry: 'It may be otherwise.'

His Lordship: 'There is no connection between the brain and the palate?'

Dr Dunn: 'It shows deficiency.'

His Lordship: 'Deficiency to the palate.'

Mr Henry: 'Supposing the prisoner had three brothers with incomplete palates, would that show some family deficiency to the organisation, mentally and bodily?'

Dr Dunn: 'Bodily, and probably mentally.'

His Lordship: 'It may be and it may not be. Don't you know many people who cannot speak plainly and yet are extremely sensible men?'

Dr Dunn: 'Yes.'

Dr Campbell, medical superintendent at Garlands Asylum, who had been 'intimately connected' with the treatment of insanity for over twenty-six years, said he had seen Wilson that morning and he considered him 'physically and mentally very ill-developed'. He was 'practically uneducated, the pupils of his eyes were more dilated than ordinary but he had no nervous manner about him'. Dr Campbell told the court, 'Wilson's memory, so far as the prisoner stated to him, was a blank in regard to New Year's Day, but in other matters seemed quite good.' There was insanity in the family: Wilson's father had a cousin in a lunatic asylum. As to the facts, counsel said there was no evidence that Wilson took the gun from upstairs, but rather from the kitchen mantelpiece. 'The poor lad was mentally deranged on New Year's Day, his mind was now blank as to what had occurred and he had no idea he had killed one of his best friends.'

Summing up, the judge said that 'every man was presumed to be sane and to possess a sufficient degree of reason to be responsible for his crimes until the contrary was proved, and that to establish a defence on the ground of insanity it must be clearly proved that at the time of committing the act, the accused was labouring under such a defect of reason from disease of the mind as not to know the nature and quality of the act he was doing, or if he did know it, he did not know it was wrong.' The jury had a straightforward choice: guilty of murder, or not guilty due to insanity. It took them twenty-five minutes to return a guilty verdict, with a recommendation to mercy 'on account of previous good character'. Passing sentence of death, the judge told Wilson, 'You had no mercy. You sent out of this world a person who had shown nothing to you but kindness and treated you with nothing but affection.' Wilson made 'no manifestation of feeling', and was removed from the court.

THE EXECUTION

The execution of Joseph Wilson was set for Tuesday 22 March 1892, three Sundays having passed since his sentence, as was the rule. Representations were made to the effect that his mental condition was such that he should not be hanged, and a petition was raised at Millom. Two 'eminent gentlemen', one an MP, urged the Home Secretary to 'invoke the clemency of the Crown', and two experts from Broadmoor and Woking attended Carlisle to examine Wilson's mental condition. Their report 'was not such as to induce the Home Secretary to interfere with the sentence'. Awaiting his fate, Wilson wished to make it known that he would never have committed the crime 'if he had been in his right senses', and expressed 'deepest sympathy' for the Crossman family.

The *Carlisle Journal* reported events: 'When the hands of the clock pointed to four minutes to eight, Billington, who had several black straps hanging over his arm, beckoned to the Governor that the time for action had arrived'. Entering the cell, he pinioned Wilson's arms, and Wilson emerged, repeating the words of the chaplain in 'firm and fervent tones'. He looked about anxiously; but walked steadily enough to the 'engine of death', the same one used to hang the infamous trio, Rudge, Martin and Baker, six years before. As he stood on the drop, Billington strapped his legs and adjusted the noose. Then he put the white hood over his head, stepped back and pulled the lever. The doors dropped with a 'startling clatter' against the sides of the pit, into which Wilson's body was then suspended. Death was reported as 'practically instantaneous', and the black flag was raised for the benefit of the assembled crowd.

THE VERDICT

Why did Joseph Wilson take a shotgun and shoot Marion Crossman, his friend and landlady? No motive was established and Wilson never offered one. It seems they had some quarrel, perhaps over breakfast or some issue that may have arisen between them. The only thing that is certain is that this was not a crime caused through alcohol; no one in the house had much, if anything, to drink the night before – New Year's Eve – or on the morning of the crime; Wilson had just a glass of beer and a glass of rum and water.

Richard Crossman was adamant that he left the gun in his bedroom before leaving the house. The two boys, John and Richard junior, saw Wilson take it from the mantelpiece in the kitchen afterwards. While there was no evidence to say that Wilson brought it downstairs, it was probably him. He loaded it with two cartridges and shot Mrs Crossman. It was not a spontaneous act. As he told PC Currie, 'I put another cartridge into the gun to make bloody well sure of her.' There was also his remark to Mrs Cole: 'Someone else will have their breakfast in another two hours.'

A medical man examined Wilson on the morning of his trial. He said Wilson's mind was blank at the time. How could he possibly know, on just one assessment? Wilson may have been suffering from stress, or he may have been angry, possibly through being jilted by Mary Ann, or maybe Marion Crossman tormented him over something. Whatever caused him to shoot her; there was no evidence that he was insane. Today, he may have been convicted of manslaughter on the grounds of diminished responsibility, an option not open to the courts at that time.

10
A WALK OF FATALITY

'Not within the memory of any who people this borough has there been a tragedy which has created such a shock, aroused such a feeling of horror and caused such a profound expression of regret.'

Thus reported the *North Western Daily Mail* in February 1901 on the murder of a young woman and the suicide of her killer, 28-year-old Arthur Thomas Cunningham.

Arthur Cunningham was a 'diminutive' man who suffered from rheumatics, and consequently was off work regularly at the Barrow shipyard where he was employed as a driller. Some three years before this tragic event on the white sands of Walney Island his wife died, leaving him to look after two daughters, the eldest of whom was nine years of age. The family had moved in with his parents in Buccleugh Street, Barrow, the previous Monday, although previously had occupied premises in Clive Street. Since his wife's untimely death, Cunningham had become quiet; he was a lonely, isolated and stooping figure when he met Rose Callow.

Rose was about Cunningham's age. She had moved to Barrow from London about two years before they met, and was employed as a domestic servant at a 'gentleman's house' in Abbey Road, although it was said that she had lately been living at Scally's Lodging House in the town. She was described as 'rather prepossessing in appearance' and of a very lively temperament. Attractive and bubbly we would say today. She and Cunningham hardly seemed suited, yet had become so attached to one another there had been rumours of marriage, indeed he had indicated as much to Julia Cunningham, his mother, 'as soon as I am better', which would not have pleased her. She objected to their liaison; she had seen them together and had said so. As the *Mail* reported, 'the temperament of the man and that of the woman were diametrically opposed', so it was not surprising that they had some disagreement in the days leading up to their deaths.

A long walk, as it happens, especially taking into account the time of year and the late hour. They were seen in Barrow, heading towards Walney Island, by a mutual acquaintance, to whom Rose remarked, 'I'm going for a sea breeze.' Evidently Rose taking a stroll on the island was not an unusual occurrence, so she would not have suspected any ill intention on behalf of

Cunningham. A policeman saw the couple in the town at 8.30 p.m., walking towards the Walney Channel, and they were seen about an hour later by another policeman, PC Postlethwaite, on the promenade on Walney Island itself, walking towards North Scale. In those pre-bridge days, they would have crossed over to the island by the ferry. Exactly what happened after the last sighting can never be known, but the following morning, at about 10 a.m., Cunningham returned to his parents' house in Buccleugh Street and told his brother, William, that he had shot Rose. William told their other brother, James, who was in bed having been at work all night.

James got up, went downstairs and asked Arthur if what he had heard was true and, if so, what he had done with the gun. Arthur said he had thrown it away. He then started crying and said to James, 'Don't tell the old people,' meaning their parents. A little later the two brothers, James and Arthur, went to the Cavendish Arms Hotel for a drink. Arthur had two small brandies, and when asked again 'if it was true', he replied that it was. 'I had nowhere to go, and Rose had nowhere to go, so I thought I'd end it. I got the revolver out of the canister and took her across to Walney and shot her. It was near to the windmill. I covered her over with my overcoat.' When they left the Cavendish Arms, Arthur said he would go home and wait for the police to come for him. James went to their sister's and told her what Arthur had told him, and when his brother-in-law arrived at the house they decided to go to Walney Island and search for the body.

Over a century ago, an old windmill stood in the present-day Mill Lane area of Walney Island. Beyond, to the north, lay 'a bleak desolate landscape of stunted grass and drifting sand and shore' – much as today, but without the airfield. There were no houses. Arthur had told James that Rose lay in a hollow, 'past the windmill'. James and his brother-in-law searched for half a mile beyond the windmill, but were unable to find Rose's body.

Having left James at the Cavendish Arms on the Saturday afternoon, Arthur Cunningham went to his parents' house, where his mother observed he appeared to be 'very depressed, as though he had some great trouble on his mind'. She said nothing to him, but at about 5 p.m., when he was pouring a cup of tea, she saw him put some powder into it. A little later she asked him where he had been as he was so dirty. He told her he had murdered Rose Callow. She thought he was joking and did not believe him. He went upstairs to bed.

An hour later she went to his bedroom where she found him lying dead on the bed, a bullet wound near his right temple. She did not hear the pistol shot, although she was in the house at the time. She knew he'd had the revolver for about a week. She called for her husband who sent for the police, and Inspector Egan and PC Duckworth attended the house. The officers found a small revolver on the floor close to the bed. Three bullets had been fired from it, although one was sufficient to kill Arthur Cunningham. Some 'crystalised substance' was found on a cloth on a table, and underneath a paper packet, the sort that wraps powder, bearing the words 'Sulphate of Zinc'. The first suicide attempt had failed – the sulphate was not sufficient to cause death – the second had not, although why Cunningham had not used the revolver in the first place isn't apparent. Maybe he dreaded the pain of a bullet, however short-lived, which an overdose of sulphate of zinc might not have given. He had been determined to take his own life, of that there was no doubt.

James Cunningham told the police of Arthur's confession: that he had murdered Rose Callow and that her body lay on Walney Island, north of the windmill. At seven o'clock the next morning, Detective Sergeant Vickers and PC Postlethwaite set out to find what James Cunningham and his brother-in-law had failed to find: Rose's body. They commenced a search of 'miles of ground', extending from south of the windmill northwards. It can't have been easy, but the policemen were determined and four hours later they found Rose. She was lying in a hole at the foot of a sandhill, on the west side of the island, two miles to the north-west of the old windmill. She lay barely fifty yards from the high water mark, still covered by Cunningham's topcoat. Her hat lay close by. There was a small bullet wound in her left temple. She would have died instantly.

Unmistakable marks in the sand indicated that a desperate struggle had taken place, both where Rose's body was discovered and at another place nearby. There was no doubt she had fought for her life. If, as was the case, Cunningham had been armed, one would have thought he could simply have shot her, and that she would not have had an opportunity to resist. One can only speculate as to what happened. Perhaps he was pointing the gun, telling her why she had to die, and she was able to grapple with him. She may have had to walk to such a remote place, so late at night, at gunpoint, and then turned on him in a futile bid for her life. We cannot know. Dr Thomas examined the bodies of both the deceased. He found that Rose Callow had been shot at point blank range. He did not consider it had been self-inflicted. That Cunningham had shot himself was not in question. Walney Island had a murder; Barrow-in-Furness had a suicide. It remained only for an inquest to be held on both parties.

After hearing the testimonies of witnesses, a pocket diary, identified as Arthur Cunningham's and containing handwriting also identified as his, was produced. The coroner read the following extracts from it: 'We have both

The dunes at Walney Island. (Paul Heslop)

made up our mind to go together'; 'You will find her by the old windmill at Walney'; 'Friday. Goodbye to all. I have been lead (*sic*) to this'; 'God bless my dear little ones. God wills, I think it must be done'. These entries indicate a suicide pact. But then, to Rose Callow's brothers, Arthur Cunningham wrote in his diary: 'Your sister was going astray, so I took the bother to shoot her'. This hardly indicates any willingness on the part of Rose to die, rather he blames her for what he perceived as her conduct, and he wanted her brothers to know about it. The jury did not accept the deaths were as a result of a suicide pact. Instead, their verdicts were that Rose Callow was 'wilfully murdered', and that Arthur William Cunningham committed suicide afterwards.

If Cunningham committed suicide through remorse or regret, then his decision may have been inevitable. If it was through fear of detection and the noose, he may yet have escaped justice, for the place where he killed Rose Callow was the perfect spot for a murder. Detective Sergeant Vickers said they were fortunate to find the body 'among the white sandhills', which in a few days would have been entirely covered by drifting sand. In such an event, Rose would have been regarded as a missing person, someone who perhaps had moved away from the area in her search for a home and happiness. There would have been no evidence of her death – save what Arthur Cunningham chose to disclose.

Victorian Barrow – the Town Hall. (Paul Heslop)

THE VERDICT

Arthur Cunningham was a quiet man who seldom spoke to anyone. As the *Mail* reported, 'the liveliness of his sweetheart would not exactly meet with his approbation'. He had on occasion seen her talking to other male acquaintances, and may have been jealous. Attractive and bubbly, Rose Callow didn't seem the sort of person who would agree to a suicide pact. Then there was the entry in Cunningham's diary, addressed to her brothers: 'Your sister was going astray, so I took the bother to shoot her'.

Here were the facts: the tragic loss of his wife; ill health and, consequentially, lack of income; no suitable home, apparently, for Arthur Cunningham and his sweetheart to live in together (assuming she wanted to, and that's not certain); a woman who chatted to other men; the acquisition of a pistol a week or so before he used it. In the depths of depression, Cunningham murdered Rose, not with any intention to get away with it, but because he saw it as the thing to do. A sad case, not least because he left behind two daughters to be looked after by ageing grandparents.

THE CRIME OF ATTEMPTED SUICIDE

Prior to 1961, it was a crime to commit suicide. This seems bizarre, since it would be impossible to prosecute anyone who succeeded. However, it was also a crime to attempt suicide, and consequently anyone who failed could find him or herself sent to prison. Since many people who attempt to take their own lives are in need of help, not punishment, one questions the wisdom of the law as it was.

It seems that commonsense prevailed in the case of Miss Clara Annie Kynoch, who had lodged with Mrs Hunter at Main Street, Ravenglass, in 1924. When Mrs Hunter went away for a while, she insisted Miss Kynoch leave the house. Miss Kynoch, nevertheless, 'effected an entry', to which Mrs Hunter did not agree. Mrs Hunter reported the matter to PC Walling, who accompanied her to the house, presumably to eject Miss Kynoch. The constable found her sitting in an outbuilding, looking quite ill, with a bottle close by. 'I have taken some spirits of salts,' she told him, adding that she had swallowed two mouthfuls. PC Walling called a doctor, who gave her an emetic (to cause vomiting), after which she was taken to hospital for 'temporary treatment'.

Miss Kynoch was charged with the crime of attempted suicide by taking poison, and appeared before the magistrates at Millom. Superintendent Melville, however, sent for Miss Kynoch's relatives, who came to the court and, having given assurance that they would look after her, and Miss Kynoch herself having promised not to attempt an overdose again, she was released without any further action. The Suicide Act of 1961 abolished the crime of suicide, and attempting to commit suicide. However, the Act made it a crime to aid, abet, counsel or procure the suicide, or attempted suicide, of another.

11

A HONEYMOON TRAGEDY

Borrowdale, 1928

Grange-in-Borrowdale, by the River Derwent, is one of the most scenic places in Lakeland. Retired farmer Tom Wilson was a lucky man indeed to be abroad in such a lovely spot on a fine June evening. It was 7.30 p.m., and as he walked through Cumma Catta woods by the river, he may have been surprised in those pre-tourism days to see someone reclining under a brown umbrella by a natural bathing pool known as Kidham Dub.

As he made his way from the riverside towards the road, Wilson saw that the umbrella covered the upper part of a woman's body. She was lying on her back, head down the incline towards the river, her knees drawn up and her legs apart. A white kid glove lay beside her, partly inside out, as though peeled from her hand. Returning to the village, Wilson mentioned his discovery to one or two of the locals, and word soon reached George Mounsey, who happened to be in company with an off-duty detective constable named Pendlebury, of Southport Police. At 8.45 p.m., they walked about 150 yards along the riverside path until they came upon the woman, still reclining under her umbrella. They could see she was of 'Chinese nationality'. They could also see that she was dead, with ligatures wrapped tightly around her neck. Her skirt and underskirt were lifted above her hips, and her underclothing was 'disarranged'. There was no sign of a struggle, although the manner in which she lay seemed to suggest sexual assault.

Pendlebury telephoned the police, and Inspector Graham of Keswick drove to the scene on his motorcycle. When he examined the body he saw there were two cords and some string tied about the woman's neck. He sent for Dr Crawford, and arranged for 'flashlight photographs'. The doctor estimated the woman had been dead for five or six hours. He noted that her ungloved left hand was curved upwards towards the shoulder, and the ring finger was marked where her ring, or rings, had been. There was no question of suicide; the woman had been murdered. But who was she?

She was 29-year-old Wai Sheung Siu Miao, a Chinese national, the daughter of a wealthy merchant who had died thee years previously. She spoke English very well, and was described as a well-travelled businesswoman, a 'very

Do you want a
GOOD INVESTMENT?
If so, you should subscribe to our
RACING LETTERS.
See Page 6.

THE ILLUSTRATED

READ OUR
CRICKET NOTES.
By AN EXPERT
See Page 6.

POLICE NEWS

LAW COURTS
AND WEEKLY RECORD
THE OLDEST AND BEST POLICE JOURNAL IN THE WORLD.
WITH WHICH IS INCORPORATED
GREAT GLOVE FIGHTS.
ESTABLISHED 1864

No. 3357. [REGISTERED AT THE G.P.O. AS A NEWSPAPER.]   THURSDAY, JUNE 28, 1928.   TWOPENCE

SCENE OF THE TRAGEDY

THE BORROWDALE VALLEY.

THE CHINESE BRIDE AND HER HUSBAND WERE SEEN WALKING.

FOUND STRANGLED.

ARREST OF THE HUSBAND.

PRETTY NEWLY MARRIED CHINESE GIRL STRANGLED IN LAKELAND

Murder in Lakeland.

generous person' who had worked with the YWCA in China. She had been married just three weeks before, in America, to Chung Yi Miao, aged 28. He was a law student who had gone to America to study at Loyola University, Chicago. Following their marriage, the couple had sailed to Glasgow, and visited Edinburgh before travelling to the Lake District, where they checked into the Borrowdale Gates Hotel, Grange, on Monday 18 June. She had travelled with jewellery, including rings and necklaces, worth £3–4,000, as well as a letter of credit for $10,000 (about £2,000). The next day the young bride was dead, apparently raped, robbed of her jewellery, and murdered. Establishing the movements of the couple on the day of the murder was vital.

They were seen to arrive at the Borrowdale Gates by Dorothy Holliday, a maid. In fact they were seen often, either in the hotel or in the area close by – hardly surprising since people of Oriental appearance would not have been a common sight in Lakeland in 1928. The gateman on the Grange–Portinscale road saw them on the Monday afternoon, when Chung, who was carrying a camera, asked him about walks in the area, and that evening they were spotted walking towards Grange Bridge. A hotel guest noticed that Wai Sheung wore two rings: a diamond solitaire and a diamond wedding ring, both on the wedding finger of her left hand.

The following day, Tuesday, Ms Holliday saw Wai Sheung come down to breakfast, followed by Chung. They were seen to go out together, arm in arm, by Holliday, she thought about two o'clock that afternoon (although it was probably earlier). He wore a blue overcoat and a grey felt hat; she had a fur coat on. Two Orientals, the man tall, the woman barely 5ft, both wearing warm clothing on a June day would have been a distinctive couple and surely would have been spotted, as they were, by several people: near Grange church between 1.30 p.m. and 2 p.m., and on Grange Bridge. William Dugdale, who was driving a charabanc from Seatoller to Keswick, saw them at the Seatoller (east) side of the bridge. Dugdale asked if they wanted to get into the bus. The man hesitated at the gate, then walked off towards Rosthwaite. The woman said, 'No.' A man and woman, who were 'obviously Orientals', were seen at a horse trough by the side of the road, walking from the direction of Grange. He was taller than her, and carried a camera. She was wearing a fur coat.

The next sighting was by Susan Cowper, who was sheltering from a shower at the Grange end of the bridge about 3 p.m. (the exact time may be inaccurate). As she waited, she saw a man 'who was not an Englishman' approaching. He was tall and very dark, and wore an overcoat. She noticed him because she had seen him the previous afternoon with a Chinese woman she took to be his wife. The woman had worn a fur coat. This time the man was alone. A moment later Addison Pepper saw a man walking alone through the village towards the Borrowdale Gates Hotel. At 4.30 p.m., or maybe earlier, Dorothy Holliday saw Chung return to the hotel alone. At 5 p.m., when she saw him in his bedroom, she asked if the lady was coming in for tea. He said his wife had gone to Keswick 'to do shopping'. He had tea alone in the dining room, and at 6 p.m., when she took some hot water to his bedroom, he said, 'My wife has not returned. She said she would be back by six.' At 7 p.m. he had dinner – alone.

Beatrice Crossley, the hotel proprietor, also saw Chung return to the hotel. He told her his wife had gone to Keswick to buy some warm underclothing

Grange Bridge and River Derwent today. (Paul Heslop)

and something for his cold. He asked her to telephone some shops about her. She said they were closed, but they could wait for the bus from Keswick, which should arrive about 9 p.m. Chung asked her to get the maid to light his bedroom fire, and this was done. Later, Holliday told him Miss Crossley had gone to the post office to telephone to find out if anyone had seen his wife. He then asked her, 'Has she gone to where they bathe?' and began striking his head, saying, 'Why doesn't she come back?' He went to bed at 10 p.m., his wife not having returned.

Miss Crossley telephoned the police, but she need not have done, for as we have seen the body of Wai Sheung had been found and the police were at the scene of the crime. Inspector Graham, having 'made enquiries', arrived at the Borrowdale Gates Hotel at 11 p.m. to find Chung in bed, wearing his pyjamas. He told him he was being detained on suspicion of murdering his wife. 'Suspicion? What do you mean by that?' asked Chung. He was handed over to two constables and taken to Keswick, while Graham searched the hotel bedroom, finding a locked jewel case, and luggage. There was a camera on the dresser. He also found two unused film cases. He locked the door and kept the key, and proceeded to Keswick police station.

At 2 a.m., at the police station, as he was being searched, Chung said, 'She had one necklace on. She had white one on yesterday afternoon. She had pocketbook with her. She had diamond ring on. Has she these with her now?' At 7 a.m., when Deputy Chief Constable Barron saw Chung in his cell, he declared, 'It is terrible, my wife assaulted, robbed and murdered.'

Dr Crawford carried out the post-mortem examination. Of the three ligatures about the neck, two were cords, one over 4ft in length, the other over 5ft. The third was a length of double twisted string, which was found under the cords and was sufficient itself to cause death. When he gave evidence at the trial, Dr Crawford gave a demonstration of how he thought the string could be applied and twisted, causing instantaneous unconsciousness. The killer had lingered after strangling her to apply more ligatures. He said Wai Sheung had been beaten about the head and face, causing blood to run from her ear, nose and mouth. Blood on the rocks meant that someone had moved the body. Chung said that any blood on his overcoat 'had been got in New York'. In fact, there was none.

Wai Shung's clothes were examined for traces of blood. The right-hand glove had 'bloodlike stains' on the thumb and all four fingers. There were blood spurt-marks on the left glove, found by the body. Human bloodstains were found on her fur coat and clothing, as well as bloody smears consistent with 'being grabbed up by a bloody hand'. Her knickers were torn, in a manner suggesting an assault, yet there was no indication of any sexual interference.

On the afternoon after Chung's arrest, his luggage was taken to Keswick police station. One item was Wai Sheung's locked jewellery case. When asked, Chung could not produce the key to it, but, searching through the luggage, Inspector Graham found a bunch of seven keys in the folds of a clean shirt in Chung's bag, almost at the bottom. One of them fitted the jewellery case, which contained jewellery to the value of £3,400. The film from Chung's camera was removed and sent for development, along with two spools containing film. Several days later, Mr W. Mayson was unrolling the spools for the purpose of developing them when Wai Sheung's diamond solitaire ring and her diamond wedding ring fell out of the second spool. They had been concealed under tinfoil and paper covering. Chung was accused of removing them from his wife's fingers after he murdered her, and secreting them into the spool where they were discovered. He may have done this to keep them, or to convince the police that a stranger had attacked his wife. When charged with her murder, Chung shook his head violently.

At Keswick Magistrates' Court, Chung's defence lawyer, Mr Thesiger, attempted to have the case dismissed at the committal stage. As well as questioning all witnesses, he had much to say to PC Scott. The officer had attended the scene, and later, in the police station, said he was asked by Chung, 'Did you see my wife?' When told he did, PC Scott said Chung asked

The newlyweds.

him, 'Had she knickers on?' 'The officer had seen the body, he must see the importance of the remark,' said Mr Thesiger. If true, it meant that Chung was asking about his wife's knickers; but no one had mentioned to Chung, at that stage, anything at all about 'knickers'. On another point, Constable Hayton said Chung asked him if the police 'had found the necklace?' But no one had told Chung a necklace was missing. Mr Thesiger suggested that the police alleged that Chung knew what only the killer could know. 'Was there anything more in this case than suspicion, conjecture and surmise?' asked Mr Thesiger. The magistrates' thought there was, and committed Chung for trial.

The following October, Chung appeared at the Cumberland Assizes. He smiled as he entered the dock, and pleaded 'not guilty' in good English. One by one the witnesses testified: to his arrival with his wife at the Borrowdale Gates Hotel on 18 June; to their walking out together the next day, and his return, alone, and more. Much was made of monetary transactions at a Glasgow bank. Perhaps the most damning thing was the circumstances in which Wai Sheung was found dead in Cumma Catta wood. Would a robber have applied three ligatures? And why were her rings found wrapped in a film spool taken from Chung's bedroom? Defence counsel said that 'the only reason Chung was arrested was that he had been out with his wife, and after that 'the police had built their case on theory'. Chung's wife was much travelled; she had gone to Keswick on her own because he had a cold. Chung had said 'necklace', not 'knickers'. PC Scott must have had the word 'knickers' on the brain, he said. Wai Sheung's satchel was missing, her money gone. Where was it? Chung didn't have it.

Testifying, Chung said he met his wife a year ago in America, where he went to study law. They married with their parents' consent. He loved his wife. He said he saw two Chinese – or maybe Japanese – men watching them, in Glasgow, Edinburgh and in Grange. He thought they were tourists. He saw his wife put the two rings into the film spool on the Tuesday morning. He could not recall if she was wearing them when they went out. She wanted to go to Keswick to shop. He kissed her as they parted. How did he know she had been 'robbed' before anyone told him? He'd said 'rudely murdered', not 'robbed'. He'd said 'necklace', not 'knickers'. He did not know a woman's undergarments were called knickers. Asked if he murdered his wife, he replied, 'What! Murder my wife? Absolutely not!'

He was asked much about his finances and the withdrawal of money from banks. When travelling, he said, he carried little money in his pockets; he handed most of it to his wife. He was asked if he and his wife went to see a doctor after they were married? Reluctantly, he admitted they did. She'd had an operation for a 'gynaecological condition' that prevented her from having sexual intercourse, or from having children. As to the keys to his wife's jewellery box, found in his possession by the police, it was possible they had fallen into his bag. As to identification, his case was supported by four witnesses who came forward on the last day of the trial to say they had seen 'two Orientals' in the area. One, Stanley Harrison, said he saw 'two Orientals' leaving Keswick railway station for Carlisle on the morning after the murder. Chung and his wife weren't the only Chinese in the area, it seems.

Defence counsel asked, reasonably, 'What was the motive?' Hardly money. Both were 'well furnished and happy'. And why would Chung come to England to murder his wife? He could have murdered her on the liner by pushing her into the sea. If they were followed, the motive must have been robbery. Where had the 'two Orientals' seen at Keswick come from? The prosecution had more to say, too. If 'the lady' had been going alone to Keswick, why was her body found on the Rosthwaite (south) side of Grange Bridge? If Chung was innocent, he would have told the police at once that he saw his wife put the rings into the film spool. 'The prisoner was the author of the crime.'

Summing up, the judge said, 'Would a robber have put string around her throat and strangled her? Only a person in whom she had confidence could be near enough to do it, and it would be unlikely that a married woman on honeymoon would have been walking with a stranger.' As he was instructing the jury, Chung shouted, 'My Lord, I am innocent!' It took the jury one hour to decide otherwise. When the court was hushed, Chung again protested his innocence, saying he had not had enough chance to say what he wanted: 'The last word I say is, I am not guilty.' The judge said he agreed with the verdict and sentenced him to death. Even as he was being taken down the steps to the cells, Chung continued shouting, 'I am not guilty.'

Chung went to the Court of Criminal Appeal, where three new witnesses testified. David Todd, of Fleetwood, and his daughter, had been on holiday. He said at 4.30 p.m. on 19 June they saw a 'foreigner' hurrying away from the direction of the Bowder Stone. He was either Chinese or Japanese. Lucy Bell, of Golders Green, London, saw 'two Orientals' between 3.30 p.m. and 4.30 p.m. that day, half a mile from the murder scene. Chung then gave a three-hour oratory, in which, among other things, he accused the trial judge of 'acting more like prosecuting counsel', and the police of 'not trying to trace the real murderer'. He said two Orientals had followed him and his wife from Glasgow. They had seen them on the bridge at Grange with a car. He

HONEYMOON MURDER.

Chinaman Convicted of Strangling his Wife.

DEATH SENTENCE PASSED.

Three Days' Trial at the Carlisle Assizes

'Sentenced to Death'. How the Cumberland News reported the conviction and sentence of Chung Yi Miao, 27 October 1928.

complained that while he languished in prison the real murderer was free. He said in Chinese law, now that his wife was dead, her property belonged to her family. This rule had been recognised for 5,000 years, so there was no point in killing her. The judge said the appeal was allowed because Chung was a native of another country. 'He has said he misunderstood, but he understood too well. This appeal is dismissed.' Chung clutched the rail of the dock for a few seconds, then turned his back on the court and was taken below.

THE EXECUTION

Chung Yi Miao was hanged at Strangeways Prison, Manchester, on 6 December 1928. In an unsubstantiated report, just before he was executed, he allegedly confessed to killing his wife. The reason, he is said to have told a reporter, was that in China a man who cannot father a son to revere his memory is 'accursed'. This 'confession' may or may not be true. Comprehensive reports on the hanging of an accused were no longer published. We cannot know what he said, or how he conducted himself at the moment of approaching death.

A Manchester solicitor, who forwarded a petition asking for a reprieve, was advised that 'the Home Secretary could not advise His Majesty to interfere with the course of the law'. On the day of execution, a small crowd gathered at the prison gates. No relatives of the condemned man were present, nor any of his friends or compatriots, possibly due to Chung professing Christianity before he died.

THE VERDICT

Chung Yi Miao was convicted on circumstantial evidence. There was nothing to connect him with the crime scene: no bloodstains, no footprints, no 'contamination' – soil, leaves, twigs on his clothing; there were no injuries to his hands consistent with punching. There was no proof at all that he was there.

Wai Sheung could have been abducted by a stranger, strangled and robbed of her jewellery and money. Several people came forward to testify, at the trial and the appeal, to say they had seen other people of Oriental appearance in the area. This evidence, it seems, carried little weight, and none at all at the appeal, when the testimony of three witnesses was brushed aside with judicial contempt. The appeal was not held on a point of law, the proper reason, but apparently to give Chung, a foreigner, every chance to put his case – then his testimony, and new evidence, were rejected.

Yet there was much to suggest Chung was the killer. He claimed his wife had gone shopping in Keswick, yet when William Dugdale stopped his charabanc and asked her if she wanted to go to Keswick, she said, 'No.' If Chung was guilty, it is submitted here that there was never a sexual assault, nor was there a robbery. Instead, after murdering his wife, he tore her knickers and took her rings from her fingers to make it appear a stranger committed the crime. It was thus premeditated, for he had the cords and string in his possession. The motive may have been her apparent inability to have children, or even sexual intercourse. If he was unaware of this before the marriage, and in the 1920s he may have been, he would have soon known about it when they were married.

The damning evidence was the rings. At his trial, Chung said his wife decided to hide them in the film spool before going for a walk. Would a newly married, much travelled, worldly woman hide her rings before stepping out in Borrowdale with her husband? And even if she did, why didn't he tell the police at the outset? If the rings were stolen by a stranger, how could they possibly be found afterwards hidden in a film spool in Chung's possession? Yet, let it be said, there was no proof she was wearing the rings when she went for that fateful walk, and until their chance discovery there was precious little evidence to incriminate Chung at all.

The verdict here is that Chung was probably guilty. Convicted of murder in a lovely Lakeland valley, his life was terminated at the end of a rope in a grim Manchester prison. One can only hope that the course of justice was accurate, and that the jury's verdict – the one that matters after all – was right.

12

SHOT IN COLD BLOOD

Newby, 1933

It was a simple, neighbourly arrangement. Thomas Parker, of Field Head Farm, who lived close to Joseph and Mary Ann Nixon of East View, would cast an eye in the direction of their isolated bungalow when he went to the outhouse where he kept his cattle; and if, perchance, the Nixons, who were elderly, were 'in any trouble', Mary Ann would hang out a white cloth so that Parker would see it. One Monday morning in February, when Parker glanced towards the Nixons' bungalow, he saw no white cloth; but neither did he see the bungalow, just the chimneystack, which was the only part of it that remained standing.

Parker had known the Nixons for over twenty years. He had visited them on Saturday evening at their bungalow, staying nearly two hours. He left Joseph Nixon in good spirits, although Mary Ann had not been feeling well. At about ten o'clock the following morning, Sunday, he had seen Joseph collecting milk from the outhouse. On the Monday morning, he could smell burning, which he put down to boys throwing the ashes of burning hay about. Then he saw the bungalow had burned down. He went to the post office and called the police.

The blaze barely attracted attention, due to the remote position of the bungalow in an area of scattered farmsteads, a scene largely unchanged today. But John Chapelhouse of Thorneywood, who lived about a mile away, was able to say that it occurred between 12.25 a.m. and 2.40 a.m. on Monday morning. Chapelhouse had returned home from Sedbergh, and after retiring to bed had heard the sound of crackling and saw a 'streak of light' at the window. He looked out and saw clouds of smoke and flames, but thinking it was a haystack on fire he went back to bed. There was no fire when he arrived home at half past midnight, he said.

When Sergeant Lilley and PC Renwick attended the scene, the bungalow, which was constructed of wood and asbestos on a brick base, was a smouldering ruin. They discovered 'certain remains' in what had been the kitchen, between the fireplace and back door. These were examined onsite by Dr Charles Thackeray, who found what he thought was a human trunk, or trunks, one with a small portion of hip bone, and vertebrae. He was unable to say whether the remains were of one body or two, or distinguish the sex of the

DOUBLE MURDER CHARGE AFTER BUNGALOW FIRE

GREAT STRICKLAND FARMER REMANDED AT SHAP

¡Neighbour Describes How He Found Footprints in Snow : Shots Heard at Night

INQUEST ON VICTIMS OPENED AND ADJOURNED

How the murders were reported in the Gazette.

Morland church. (Paul Heslop)

deceased. The police found several items: a watch, a metal ruler, a pocketknife and the blade of a razor. William Alderson, the Nixon's son-in-law, identified the ruler as one he had given to Joseph Nixon. He was uncertain about the watch. He thought the razor was one Nixon had used to 'cut his corns'. Alderson's wife, Annie, their adopted daughter, fancied she could identify the ruler and razor. Joseph and Mary Ann Nixon were both 76 years old. That they had perished in the fire seemed certain. Their remains were interred at St Laurence's churchyard, Morland, on 3 March.

If the police thought the blaze was down to a tragic accident, they would have cause to think again. William Milner, a farmer, reported that he was tending some sheep in a field near Newby at about six o'clock on Sunday evening, when he heard two gunshots coming from the direction of the bungalow. He turned to his wife and said, 'Fancy. I wonder what Joe's found to shoot tonight?' There was no one about, nor could they see the bungalow due to a high fence that obstructed their view. The shots, Milner said, were 'five or ten seconds apart'. He knew Joseph Nixon had a gun, but hadn't heard him use it for about a year.

In fact, two dreadful, cold-blooded murders had been committed, and some time afterwards the Nixons' bungalow had been set ablaze, probably in an attempt to destroy the evidence. Police made an early arrest, Richard Hetherington, aged 36, a bachelor who lived with his mother and sister on a small farm, three miles from Newby. He was brought before the magistrates the next day. The charges were that he 'feloniously, wilfully and with malice aforethought did kill and murder Joseph Nixon, and Mary Ann Nixon, between 10 a.m. on Sunday 19th, and 9 a.m. on Monday 20th February.'

The committal was heard in the magistrates' court at Hackthorpe. As well as the metal ruler and razor found in the debris, the court was told the blade of a large knife had also been found, which Joseph Nixon had carried in his pocket. Heel and toe plates and a number of eyelets from boots, items that would not burn, were found in the place he would have sat. There were charred bones, and corsets, and on the threshold of the backdoor a bloodstained sack, which had been used as a doormat. Significantly, outside the backdoor were two cartridge wads.

Dr Faulds, the pathologist, had examined the charred bodies. There were two, 'presumably one male and one female'. He described them in gruesome detail. Over 200 shot pellets were found in the male. Death was due to a gunshot wound, which had punctured the lungs and heart. Twenty-five pellets were found in the heart of the female, causing her death. If the shots heard by Mr and Mrs Milner were those that killed the Nixon's, the murder must have been committed at about six o'clock on Sunday evening and some person – probably the killer – must have returned after midnight and set fire to the bungalow.

The court was told that there was 'bad feeling' between Hetherington and Joseph Nixon due to a dispute over 'occupation of some land and money matters', and Nixon had placed the matter in the hands of his solicitor. In a letter to him, Hetherington was informed that if he did not pay £49 9s by 20 February there would be legal proceedings. The previous October, PC Renwick had seen Hetherington, at Nixon's request, about his conduct at the bungalow. Hetherington told the constable that Nixon was trying to claim more money from him than was due. The constable told him he was not 'settling a dispute with an old man in the proper manner', and warned him about his conduct. In times when policemen worked their 'patch', and were stationed throughout the village communities, it was small wonder they quickly identified a likely suspect.

At 9 p.m. on the Tuesday evening, the day after the murders, Superintendent Eccles, Sergeant Lilley and PC Bryson saw Hetherington in the barn near his house at Great Strickland. When asked if he knew anything about the fire, he replied, 'Just what people have told me.' What people? He was asked. 'Mr Wilson at Penrith Auction Mart,' he replied. He denied having a gun. Accounting for his movements on the Sunday night, he said he'd had supper with Mr Wilson, of Towcett. He stayed for two hours, went to Bedlingsgate and returned home by Little Strickland. He admitted he'd been at the bungalow on the Saturday evening, but the Nixons had apparently gone to bed. Hetherington did not want to go into his house with the police as it might upset his mother. But Superintendent Eccles went inside and saw Mrs Hetherington, who brought down a stock and hand-grip of a gun, and a box of cartridges. Eccles returned to the barn and said, 'I have the gun, where is the barrel?' Hetherington replied, 'In a box upstairs.' They went into the house but could not find it. 'It is in the barn among the hay,' said Hetherington. They moved the hay but still could not find it. Tamar Hetherington, Richard's sister, appeared, and asked him where he had got the gun. He replied, 'I found it on the roadside. I didn't want to leave it there for the bairns to pick up.'

Superintendent Eccles told Hetherington he was taking him to Shap. Hetherington said, 'I never done it.' He struggled violently, and had to be handcuffed and 'practically carried' to a motor vehicle. Then the barrel for the gun was found in a box 'at the top of the house'. A wallet was also found in his possession. It contained three letters, four receipts and an old envelope. The letters dealt with the purchase and construction of the bungalow at East View – the Nixons' home. The envelope was addressed to Mr N. Hodgson, at Penrith, a friend of Joseph Nixon, whose handwriting it was.

The gun was purchased on 17 February in Penrith, at a sports shop owned by Walter Wilkinson, who identified Hetherington as the man who bought it. When the gun barrel was examined, human blood was found on it. There was also blood on the box of cartridges. More blood was discovered on a pair of corduroy trousers Hetherington had worn on 19 February, which Superintendent Eccles found at the bottom of a tin box.

HD 086677

CERTIFIED COPY of an
Pursuant to the Births and

ENTRY OF DEATH
Deaths Registration Act 1953

				Registration District	West Ward			
1933.	Death in the Sub-district of	Morland			in the County of Westmorland			

Columns: -	1	2	3	4	5	6	7	8	9
No.	When and where died	Name and surname	Sex	Age	Occupation	Cause of death	Signature, description, and residence of informant	When registered	Signature of registrar
12	Nineteenth February 1933 at East View Newby R.D	Joseph Nixon	Male	76 years	Farmer	From gunshot wounds not self inflicted criminal proceedings taken against Richard Hetherington for murder of deceased conviction of murder no PM	Certificate received from John Richardson coroner for county of Westmorland Inquest held February 23rd 1933 and by adjournment on 30th June 1933 when verdict found	Seventh July 1933	Ernest Jackson
									Registrar.

Certified to be a true copy of an entry in a register in my custody.

Elizabeth Thoele   Superintendent Registrar

7th March 2007   Date

CAUTION: THERE ARE OFFENCES RELATING TO FALSIFYING OR ALTERING A CERTIFICATE AND USING OR POSSESSING A FALSE CERTIFICATE. ©CROWN COPYRIGHT
WARNING: A CERTIFICATE IS NOT EVIDENCE OF IDENTITY.

Death certificate for Joseph Nixon. (Penrith Register office)

Ralph Powley, farmer, said he saw Hetherington walking towards the bungalow on the Saturday evening. Hetherington told him he was going to Joe Nixon's, as he was 'having a bit of bother with him'. He saw him again the following morning, when Hetherington said he had called at the bungalow but had not seen Nixon as there was 'not a soul astir'. The fire had been flickering in the grate and he tried the door twice, but then came away. He said Nixon was trying to claim money from him, which was not due, and threatened 'to put him in the reservoir', which Nixon himself had built next to the bungalow. George Wilson, the Towcett farmer, said Hetherington visited his house on Sunday 19 February, arriving at 7.30 p.m. He left at about 11.30 p.m. After the magistrates committed Hetherington for trial, he said, 'I plead not guilty. I shall reserve my defence to the trial.' His solicitor added, 'He wishes to say he has never used a gun in his life.' This final remark was not supposed to include, presumably, the period of service Hetherington spent in the army in the Great War, when he was wounded at Cambrai.

The trial took place at the Shire Hall, Appleby, in May. Hetherington pleaded not guilty. Sir Walter Greaves-Lord, prosecuting, admitted the evidence was 'entirely circumstantial'. So it was: no one saw the murders committed, no one saw who set the house ablaze and there was no direct evidence to connect Richard Hetherington with the scene on either occasion. But there was evidence, nonetheless, against him – not least that Hetherington had bought a gun just two days before the murders, and that he had lied about this, and the wallet containing personal papers in Joseph Nixon's handwriting, which was found in his possession.

Apart from the evidence heard at the committal, there was more at the trial. Nelson Hodgson said he saw Hetherington at Penrith Auction Mart in January, when Hetherington told him, 'I will finish old Joe.' Ernest Johnson, for solicitors at Penrith, confirmed that a letter was sent to Hetherington in January, claiming £49 9s for rent due for keeping sheep and cattle, and threatening proceedings for recovery of the money. Hetherington had replied, denying there was any claim on him, and that he had claim upon Nixon for what he had done on his land. In another letter to the solicitors, Hetherington claimed Nixon had poisoned hens that he (Hetherington) had bought for him, and that Nixon had thrown the hens onto his land. This letter had been received just two days before the murders. The disputes between the two men were apparent; there was bad blood, without doubt.

George Wilson, the Towcett farmer, reiterated that Hetherington visited his house at 7.30 p.m. on the Sunday and had supper with him. When Hetherington left at 11.30 p.m. he was 'perfectly normal'; there was nothing to suggest he had committed a double murder. Stanley Turner, who was also present, said Hetherington had worn corduroy trousers. Eva Balmer, a servant at Bedlandgate, saw a man with a limp pass her on the Strickland road at about 11.15 p.m. He was coming from the direction of Towcett. She knew Hetherington, and knew also that he had a limp. She saw him in darkness, so may not have recognised his face. She said he appeared to have something dark under his arm – a shotgun, perhaps. Dr Faulds, the pathologist, confirmed that in each case death was caused by gunshot wounds. He also examined the corduroy trousers, the sack used as a doormat, the gun barrel and cartridges, all of which were bloodstained. It was human blood, he said, and stained relatively recently. Walter Wilkinson, the gunsmith who sold Hetherington the gun and cartridges, said that when he produced the gun, Hetherington came behind the counter, as though to avoid being observed.

Testifying, Hetherington said he had joined the army at nineteen and was wounded in the right shoulder. This affected the movement of his arm. He admitted 'having disagreements' with Joseph Nixon, but denied owing him money. In fact, Nixon owed him money, he said. 'Did you shoot Mr and Mrs Nixon?' he was asked. 'No,' he replied, saying he had never been in trouble before except for riding a bike without a light. He admitted buying the gun in Penrith, saying he had seen others poaching and he thought he had as much right to a rabbit or two. When he got home he hid the gun because he did not want his family to know he had been poaching. He took it into the house to prevent the children finding it.

He said that on the Saturday before the murders he went to the Nixons' bungalow, but they had evidently gone to bed. On the roadside he picked up some papers (the letters) and put them in his pocket. He thought he would return them to Mr Nixon the following Tuesday at Penrith market. His remark to Powley about putting Nixon in the reservoir was a joke. On Sunday he left the house at about 5.45 p.m. He wore corduroy trousers. He never went near the bungalow that night, but went to George Wilson's where he remained until 11.30 p.m. He arrived home at about 12.10 a.m.

Hetherington's counsel told the court he would produce evidence of alibi. He would prove Hetherington left home at 6.15 p.m. on the evening of the murders, without a gun. It was five miles to the Nixon's bungalow, so it was impossible to reach it before 6 p.m. Two witnesses were called: John Hetherington, aged 10, was the first. He was Hetherington's nephew. He said he saw his 'Uncle Dick' at a quarter to six on the night of the murders. He knew the time because he looked at the clock. 'Who told you you were coming here to say you looked at the clock?' he was asked by prosecuting counsel. 'My auntie,' replied the boy. Naivety and innocence: two ingredients that ensured a truthful reply! Tamar Hetherington was next. She said she saw her brother (the accused) at 5.45 p.m. on the Sunday evening. Sergeant Lilley said Tamar Hetherington had told him her brother had left the house 'after tea', at about 4 p.m. Now, at the trial, she was saying otherwise.

Mr Jackson, for Hetherington, told the jury, 'We have come to the closing scenes of one of the greatest dramas which has ever happened in this county. The prisoner was not shaken one iota by cross-examination.' Accounting for the bloodstains, they came about because he had sustained an injured shoulder during the war, and when firing at rabbits the gun hit his nose, which bled. He wiped the blood on his trousers, and put his left hand on the gun for another shot where the bloodstains were found. 'There is not one tittle of evidence that he was anywhere near the bungalow.' Mere suspicion would not do, Mr Jackson told the court.

The prosecution dismantled Hetherington's alibi. 'The evidence to prove he was not at the bungalow came from his own home.' The little lad was saying what he had been told to say. His sister changed her mind about the time he left the house. The judge said the old couple were living in such a way that it was difficult to imagine anyone being minded to murder them. It is submitted here that the crux of the case was the gun and the contents of the wallet; Joseph Nixon's papers were found in Hetherington's possession. The jury took three hours to reach a guilty verdict. Hetheringon did not flinch. When the judge said, 'You shall hang by the neck until you are dead;' he nodded his head and left the court without a word.

THE EXECUTION

Hetherington's defence indicated there would be an appeal. But there was no appeal. Instead, his solicitor sent a petition to the Home Secretary for a reprieve on the grounds of the condemned man's 'mental condition'. It was refused. Hetherington spent his final days playing table games with his captors. His cell was known as the 'luxury suite' because it had two rooms and a bathroom. From the latter a secret door led to the final place of his life's journey, the execution shed.

On the morning of the execution, 20 June 1933, about a hundred people gathered at the gates of Walton Prison, Liverpool. 'A deep silence fell over them' as eight o'clock approached. A white-haired man stepped out of the crowd and took off his cap. Kneeling down, he crossed himself. He did not know Hetherington, he said, but thought he should say a short prayer for him. At 8.05 a.m. two death notices were fastened to the prison gates: the Sheriff's Notice, with worthies' names certifying 'judgement of death', and another, signed by the prison surgeon, certifying that he had examined the body and he found that Richard Hetherington was dead. Capital punishment, insofar as events were reported to the public, and the massed crowds that had once gathered to witness justice take its course, had certainly changed.

THE VERDICT

The murder of Joseph Nixon was premeditated. Richard Hetherington bought the gun and ammunition just two days before calmly walking to the isolated bungalow and shooting him. He may not have planned or even wanted to kill Mary Ann Nixon, but would have considered he had no choice. He could hardly have spared her and expected to escape detection. One imagines the scene: the elderly couple facing the man with the shotgun, remonstrating, pleading, begging him to spare their lives. But unknown forces drove Hetherington: hate, anger, stress. Who knows?

One imagines, too, his brain working overtime afterwards. How to get rid of the evidence? Go and set fire to the place! So he did, in vain, for he had not the cunning to commit the perfect crime. One wonders if his wartime service in France played a part in his judgement, or his mental state? His defence team may have wanted to introduce this in mitigation; but they could only do so if he admitted killing Joseph and Mary Ann. It was acquittal they sought, total and absolute. A convincing alibi was the key, so they called upon his sister to lie about the time he left the family home that fateful evening, and his 10-year-old nephew, who was told to say he 'looked at the clock'. It didn't wash with the jury. Richard Hetherington murdered two elderly people in cold blood. He was rightly convicted.

13

A FRENZIED ATTACK

St Bees, 1950

The first indication that all was not well at Mrs Laura Buller's house in Main Street, St Bees, was at about 10.45 p.m. one February evening when the next-door neighbour, Thomas Park, heard strange noises which sounded to him like 'someone trying to break a block of wood with an axe by bumping the wood on the floor'. The next-door neighbour on the other side of Mrs Buller's, Ada Dodding, had heard the bumping too. They lasted for about half an hour, she said. At ten o'clock the following morning, when a light in Mrs Buller's house was still burning and there was no response to their knocking, Mr Park called the police.

PC Atkinson lived but a few yards away, and a few minutes later he too was knocking on Mrs Buller's door. Mrs Buller was 66 years of age, a retired music teacher, who had lived alone in her terraced house at St Bees for three years. She was regarded as eccentric, and now good neighbours and a policeman were concerned about her welfare. Receiving no reply to his knock, PC Atkinson forced an entry into the house, where he found Mrs Buller lying on the floor, naked except for her stockings, 'violently done to death by some man, who, with maniacal frenzy, broke many of her ribs and other bones', as prosecuting counsel would tell the jury at Cumberland Assizes the following May. Mrs Buller's clothing was strewn about the floor, but there were no signs of ransacking and nothing had been stolen.

Dr Faulds, pathologist, attended the house, where he saw Mrs Buller's body in situ. She had extensive injuries to her head and body, scratches consistent with nail marks around her neck and nine small cuts on the left shoulder consistent with biting. The body was taken to Whitehaven Hospital, where Dr Faulds carried out a post-mortem examination, which revealed the hyoid bone in the throat, eighteen ribs and the sternum (breastbone) had been fractured. Sexual intercourse had taken place. 'She died from asphyxia from compression of the chest and neck,' said Dr Faulds. The weight of a body kneeling on Mrs Buller's chest would have been sufficient to cause death, he added.

The 'bumpings' heard by Mrs Buller's neighbours were obviously down to whatever Laura Buller's killer was doing with her in the course of raping and murdering her. It was a frenzied attack, and the police were anxious to apprehend her killer as soon as possible. He was identified almost

The Manor House Hotel, St Bees; formerly the Royal Oak Inn. (Paul Heslop)

immediately, despite having fled the area. In fact, the police had not far to look to discover how Laura Buller had met her fate. She had been seen talking to a man just down the street at the Royal Oak Inn (now the Manor House Hotel) on the night of her death, Thursday 9 February 1950, and soon afterwards she had been seen with him again, walking towards her house.

The amount of information the police were able to disclose about the man was quite astonishing, and immediately after the crime the *Whitehaven News* published the following description: 'Patrick Ridge, aged 38, height 5ft 8ins, dark hair parted on side, high cheek bones, lantern jawed, ruddy complexion. Wearing a blue serge suit with blue polo-necked pullover, brown shoes with rubber soles and heels; may have tattoos on both forearms. A native of Kilkerrin, Carna, Galway, Eire...'. They also learnt that he enlisted in the Royal Irish Fusiliers in June 1934, army number 6977724; that in July 1944 he transferred to the King's Own Scottish Borderers, and two months later to the Royal Northumberland Fusiliers. He was discharged from the army as unfit in September 1945. The police hoped that someone who had served with Ridge would kindly supply them with a photograph, and went on, courtesy of the newspaper, to specify with great accuracy where he had served: Palestine, India, Malaya and north-west Europe, finally being sent to a military hospital in Surrey, from where he was discharged. From 1946 he had worked at 'various public works' in or near London until the previous September, when he came to work at Sellafield atomic power plant. He was billeted at Nethertown Camp until the night of the crime, but when the police arrived to arrest him he had already fled, leaving behind only his ration book.

Laura Isabella Buller was a native of Whitehaven, the only child of Mr and Mrs Wilson, who had a music shop in Lowther Street. She had had a private education, and trained as a musician. A friend, tracked down by the *Whitehaven News*, said of her, when she was a young girl, 'When she was singing in the drawing room at home, crowds of people would line the opposite side of the street to listen to her.' She became an accomplished pianist, and after leaving home to become a professional musician she married Arthur Cressey Buller, a professional dancer and singer, who said, when he learned of her death, that she 'did go in for spiritualism'. They had parted and she had lived in London, but had returned to Cumberland during the Blitz with a Mr Cope, with whom she lived at St Bees. Mr Cope died, leaving her alone with little money and in fear of becoming destitute. To earn a little extra she gave music lessons at her home in St Bees, and in Whitehaven, under the name 'Madame Laura Buller, I.R.A.M.'. This was the woman so brutally murdered in her own home by Patrick Ridge – and now the police had to find him.

The police had reason to believe Ridge had travelled by train from Barrow to London on the Friday night, after the crime. In the event, he avoided capture for ten days, until he was arrested – not in London, but in Northamptonshire, thanks to an alert policeman, PC Deaton. PC Deaton was on patrol when he saw a man walking on the road about three miles from Northampton. He was wearing a blue suit and jersey, and having seen the description of the man wanted for killing Mrs Buller he challenged him and asked him to produce his identity card. The man replied, 'I'm sorry, I haven't got it with me.' When asked his name, he replied, 'Patrick Ridge.' Ridge was arrested and brought to Whitehaven. Between arrest and his incarceration at Whitehaven, Ridge spoke not a single word, except when charged with murder, he replied, 'I have nothing to say.'

The link between Laura Buller and Ridge seems to have been one of money. She, apparently, was looking for a lodger, while he was fed up with living at Nethertown Camp. As he told Daniel Cassidy, a labourer at the Sellafield works, he was going to 'try and get lodgings with the schoolteacher woman'. He did not like the camp, and if he could not get lodgings he was going to 'lift his cards'. On that fateful Thursday evening, another work colleague, John Fleck, a joiner at Sellafield, who slept in the same room as Ridge, lent Ridge his duffle coat because it was raining. Ridge went out, wearing a blue suit and blue roll-necked pullover. By midnight, when Fleck went to sleep, Ridge had still not returned.

The licensee's wife at the Royal Oak, Mabel Marston, said Ridge came to the hotel at about 7 p.m. and consumed a pint of beer, some rum and some cheese sandwiches. Mrs Buller arrived at about 7.20 p.m. and had a glass of stout, then left. Ridge followed her out about five minutes later. Harold Marston said he heard Mrs Buller say to Ridge, 'You didn't come back when you said you would'. Ridge said he was too busy. They were clearly acquainted. At about 7.50 p.m. Nancy Braithwaite was delivering election leaflets when she saw Mrs Buller walking up to her house with a man she could not identify. He was wearing a light coat. Later, at about 9 p.m., Ridge returned to the Royal Oak, alone, and asked for a half-sized bottle to be filled with rum. He paid for it and left. Later still the same evening Jane Hodgson, of the Oddfellows Arms, served 'a man wearing a duffle coat' with £1 worth of rum in a half-sized Haig whisky bottle. It seems Ridge had plenty to drink that Thursday night.

At 6.15 a.m. the following morning, John Fleck, Ridge's roommate, woke up to find his duffle coat lying on the next bed. It was soaking wet. He saw Ridge, and when he asked him about his coat Ridge laughed. Fleck noticed Ridge's bed had not been slept in, but now Ridge went to his bed and slept. Later, police went to the hut and took possession of Ridge's clothing and the duffle coat, and handed them in for forensic examination. Some of the clothing was bloodstained. At 2.10 p.m. on Friday afternoon, Ridge gave in his notice at Sellafield. He was given the pay owing to him at 4 p.m. He was a fugitive until his arrest in Northamptonshire.

After being charged, Ridge was remanded to Durham Prison, where he had a conversation with a fellow inmate, John Woulfe. Testifying at Ridge's trial, Woulfe, hardly a man one would expect to help the prosecution, nevertheless had something interesting to say. After Ridge had told him he was in 'for murder', Woulfe asked him whom he had murdered. 'A woman in Cumberland,' Ridge replied, adding that he could not account for himself between 10 p.m. that night (of the murder) and 5 a.m. the next morning. The defence wanted to know if Woulfe had heard about another case where two men were accused of shooting a cinema manager, and asked if he was being helpful in order to get remission from his sentence. 'I thought it was the proper thing to do,' replied Woulf. The judge suppressed the inevitable laughter.

Whatever vestige of hope Ridge may have had for acquittal was crushed by the half-sized Haig whisky bottle and two glass tumblers which were found in Mrs Buller's house. All three items bore his fingerprints. From the testimonies of witnesses, in St Bees and at Nethertown Camp, and John Woulfe, as well as the bloodstained clothing and fingerprints: was there any point

The house where Laura Buller lived – and was murdered.
(Paul Heslop)

on which Ridge's defence could raise to secure acquittal for murder? There was: Mr Rowson, defence counsel, declared that he would ask for a 'special verdict' – that Ridge was not guilty of murder through schizophrenia. The man had a split personality, he said.

Dr William Haig, who had also attended Mrs Buller's house, was asked if he had ever heard of schizophrenia, 'a kind of disease that would throw a person off his balance without any warning'. Dr Haig replied that a person suffering from the disease could do sudden acts of a violent nature. He was asked if he knew what catatonic schizophrenia was. Dr Haig replied that he had no experience of it in his practice, and that his knowledge of it was from books. It seems a GP, called to testify on his findings at a crime scene, was suddenly and unexpectedly being asked, as an expert, on a disease that was comparatively unknown at the time. Mr Rowson then tried his luck with Dr Joseph Braithwaite, medical superintendent at Garlands Hospital, Carlisle, and 'a specialist in mental diseases'.

'At the present time,' said Dr Braithwaite, 'Ridge is certifiable as a person of unsound mind.' He had examined him the day before, and gained from him something of his history. Apparently, after leaving school, Ridge worked on a farm for two years. At 18 he joined the Irish Army but spent most of his time in detention. In 1934 he joined the British Army and saw service overseas, where he felt everyone was against him. In 1944 he was transferred to France, but became ill and was sent to the Surrey hospital from which he was discharged as a catatonic schizophrenic, 'a disease where there are often hallucinations during which a person imagines he hears and sees things which are not there'.

He went on, 'Ridge told me that he heard voices talking to him from time to time, and sometimes, when walking down the street, he heard voices "from the other side" talking about him. Sometimes these voices came from the other world and called him bad names.' Dr Braithwaite called these voices 'insane hallucinations'. At Sellafied, Ridge did not get on with the other men. 'He thought they were ganging up to attack him, but he could not give any reason for believing this.' Ridge had seen Mrs Buller on two occasions: the first time at St Bees, when he asked if she could give him lodgings and she told him to come back the following week, and the second on the night of the murder. 'He went to her house where they drank rum. She questioned him about his family, and asked if he would like to see his dead parents.' Ridge replied, 'I don't believe in things like that'. But then told the court, 'I saw my mother and father quite clearly and do not remember anything after that'. 'This is consistent with a man suffering from schizophrenia,' said Dr Braithwaite, adding that Ridge thought the police, the priests and the prison doctor were all against him, but these were delusions. 'Ridge did not care if he was dead tomorrow. He did not think he would be any good to himself or anyone else. He would be unable to control his desire to attack Mrs Buller because of his schizophrenic condition.' All this from a man who had seen Patrick Ridge only once – the day before his trial.

Dr M. Williams, Medical Officer of Durham Prison, said Ridge had been on remand at Durham, where he had been 'under observation' day and night. He had had five interviews with him. Dr Williams was asked if Ridge would have known the 'nature and quality' of what he did on 9 February? He replied, 'I think he would be capable of realising whether anything he did was wrong. I see no reason to think his condition would be very much different at that time.' He knew the nature and quality of what he was doing? 'Judging by his condition when I saw him, he did.'

'The question of insanity,' said the judge 'is one which has disturbed the courts for a considerable time.' There were two forms of insanity, he said: one where the accused did not know the nature and quality of the act, the other where he did know, but did not know what he was doing was wrong. 'Some insane people commit crimes with full knowledge and intent, very cleverly and with much cunning and doubling up on their tracks.' The jury, blessed with the clarity of these words, took 45 minutes to find Ridge guilty of murder. He was sentenced to death.

THE VERDICT

Patrick Ridge was to be hanged at Durham, but following a medical enquiry into his mental state the Home Secretary, James Chuter Ede, advised the King to respite the capital sentence and Ridge was instead sent to Broadmoor Institution. This may have been a fair conclusion to this case. But one hesitates...

Ridge was 'medically examined' the day before his trial. It is submitted here that a medical examination should be made over a period, and the findings not simply rest on whatever the accused says just before his trial, such as 'I hear voices from the other side', meaning 'I'm mad and can't be hanged, doctor'. At least the Home Secretary's recommendation was made after a more protracted and accurate assessment of Ridge's state of mind. One hopes so, anyway.

Just the same, one wonders: during the evening leading up to this dreadful crime, Patrick Ridge probably consumed at least one pint of beer and up to two half-bottles of rum, maybe more. Then afterwards, when he returned to his lodgings, he calmly went to sleep, then quit his job and took a southbound train. Schizophrenia? Or out of his skull through booze, a drunken wastrel who raped and crushed an old lady to death in a frenzied attack before taking flight. How strange that he didn't, apparently, suffer from schizophrenia when he was sober. The jury was unconvinced about his hearing 'voices from the other side'. They probably decided that drink – the cause of so much violent crime – and not schizophrenia or mental illness, caused Patrick Ridge to kill Laura Buller. Who would disagree?

14
THE LAST TO HANG

Workington, 1964

'Honour among thieves' is an age-old expression, which, however well known, is hardly accurate. Not in the experience of this writer, anyway. 'I'm no grass, guv', is heard often enough by investigating detectives, but when things get 'on top' there's usually not much in the way of 'honour' flying about. Saving one's own skin takes priority, as it did in the case of two unemployed dairymen, petty criminals both, who took it upon themselves one night to call on John Alan West (known as Jack) whom, they believed, had money 'lying about' in his house.

Jack West, a van driver, lived in a semi-detached council house at Seaton, near Workington. He was 53 years old, a single man who lived alone. He was at home, minding his own business, when his visitors arrived in a stolen car at about 3 a.m. on Monday 6 April 1964. Murder was committed, some of Mr West's property was stolen and evidence incriminating his attackers was left behind by two bungling, cowardly fools. But if the case itself was not of particular significance in the annals of police investigation, it merits scrutiny for two reasons: that the 1957 Homicide Act had abolished the death penalty for murder, except in certain circumstances, including, significantly, murder committed in the course of or furtherance of theft; and the guilty men would be the last two persons to lawfully hang in this country, at the same time but in different prisons, on 13 August 1964.

Mr West had lived alone in the house since the death of his mother. He was a subdued man who kept himself to himself. His house was well kept, and he always dressed well. He was a 'Gold Medal' employee of Lakeland Laundries Limited, for whom he had been employed for 35 years, and in 1954 had been awarded a gold wristwatch, which was engraved with his name. It would play an important part in the fate of Mr West's assailants, for it had been stolen and it was identifiable.

Mr and Mrs Fawcett lived next door to Jack West. They were in bed when Mr West's visitors arrived, and were awakened by heavy thuds. As Mr Fawcett got out of bed he heard the sound of a car engine starting up. Looking out of the window, he saw a car speeding off towards the main road. He and his wife then dressed and went across the road to Mr Lister's house, and Mr Lister called the police.

At 3.30 a.m. Sergeant James Park got the message to attend Mr West's house. Using a key given to him by Mr Fawcett, he went inside and found Mr West's bloodied body lying at the bottom of the stairs. As the judge at the subsequent appeal against conviction of his killers said, 'A more brutal murder it would be difficult to imagine.' Mr West had been stabbed through the heart, and beaten about the head and shoulders with a metal tube encased in a rubber sheath. His attackers had fled. The motive for the crime was not known, although robbery was rightly suspected. There was no sign of the knife used to murder Mr West in the house.

In keeping with common practice, a senior CID officer was called to the murder scene. Detective Inspector John Gibson arrived at 4.30 a.m. He saw there was blood on the side of the stairs and all the way up the staircase. The police found the rubber-covered bar, or pipe, used to strike Mr West. The following day, when the house was being forensically examined, DI Gibson found a raincoat draped over a chair in one of the bedrooms. In the pocket was a key wallet containing a medallion inscribed 'G.O. Evans' and an army memo form with the name and address of a woman who lived in Liverpool. She was a former girlfriend of Gwynne Owen (Sandy) Evans, aged 24, whose present address she did not know but whom the police traced to Clarendon Street, Preston, the address of Peter Anthony Allen, 21, who lived there with his wife, Mary, and two small children. Evans was born at Maryport. He had moved in as a lodger with the Allens the previous November. The social and domestic arrangements of Allen, his wife and Evans are uncertain; what is certain are the events that unfolded on that April night in 1964, when Allen and Evans decided to drive to Jack West's home, seeking a loan of £100 from him, or maybe to rob him. Evans believed he kept money in the house, so either option would suit their purpose. Bizarrely, while the two men were robbing and murdering Mr West in his home, Mary Allen and her two children were waiting outside in the car.

The stolen car, that is, belonging to a Mr David Cook, in which they drove to Mr West's house, arriving shortly after 2 a.m. Exactly what happened thereafter will never be known, since the only people who knew, each told his own version of events in a desperate attempt to avoid the noose. Each knew they would hang if convicted of murder if stolen property was found in their possession, or was proven to have been used by one of them – Mr West's gold watch, and two bankbooks, issued by the Workington branch of the Trustee Savings Bank.

The day after the crime, 7 April, a man purporting to be 'Mr A. West', accompanied by a 'young lady', went to the Trustee Savings Bank in Liverpool and produced the two stolen bankbooks. 'Do you think you could give me £5 from each account?' the man enquired. 'I don't see why not,' said the manager, who completed the necessary paperwork and handed him the money. The next day the forms arrived at the Workington branch and the police were called. A stolen watch, and now money obtained by deception. Our murderers were fulfilling all the necessary requirements to hang them.

Bank withdrawal receipt for £5, made in Liverpool. (By permission of Cumbria Constabulary)

On 8 April, following police enquiries, Peter Allen was arrested at his home in Preston and taken to Workington. That same afternoon Evans and Mary Allen were arrested in Manchester. In Evans' possession was a stolen driving licence in the name of 'David Cook', which he said he had found in Preston and was going to hand in to the police. Mr West's gold watch was found in the lining of his jacket. He said he had bought it from a man in Preston. He and Mary Allen were also taken to Workington. Meanwhile, at the scene of the crime, £26 was found in the airing cupboard. Evans's assumption that 'Jack West had money' was correct.

Allen was the first to be questioned by detectives. 'You can get a stack of Bibles and pile them up to here,' he said. 'Then I will stand on them and swear I know nothing about it.' He told them he and his wife had been in Liverpool at the time, looking for somewhere to live. When told his wife and Evans had also been arrested and were on their way to Workington for questioning, he struck the desk with his fist and declared, 'All right. I will tell you all. I would like to tell the whole flipping world about it.' He said the car was stolen in Preston on the Monday night, and that while he and Evans were in Mr West's house the light suddenly went out, and he started hitting out blindly. He then went upstairs 'to see if there was any cash lying about, but there wasn't,' so he grabbed some letters and two bankbooks. He claimed Evans had entered the house first, and then he went inside and went upstairs. 'As I got near the top, Mr West came out of the bedroom, made a lunge at me and I panicked. I hit him in the face with my fists... I remember seeing Gwynne hit him with the rubber tubing... It started off as an innocent robbery,' he added, as though in mitigation.

Evans said that when they arrived at Seaton they 'found Jack up'. He knocked at the front door, and Jack came downstairs and let him into the house. When they were talking there was a knock at the door, and Jack went to open it. He saw Allen hitting Jack with something in a corner, by the stairs.

He shouted, 'For Christ's sake, stop it', but Allen said, 'He's got cash and I want it'. Evans admitted he had left his raincoat and keys behind, adding, 'If I had wanted to I could have said they had been stolen, but I just want to get this off my chest.' In a statement, he added, 'I do not have to use a knife to kill a man. I am an expert in judo and karate. Peter did all the hitting... I took the watch from the kitchen table.' He said Allen burned his bloodstained shirt and the bankbooks at the Preston house. Neither man admitted stabbing Mr West. The knife had not been found, but it would be.

At 1.15 a.m. on 9 April, Allen and Evans were charged with murder 'against the peace of our sovereign lady the Queen'. Each was invited to write a reply. Allen wrote: 'I would like to say I am very sorry for all I have done'. Evans: 'I want to appoligze [sic] for all the inconvence [sic] we have caused and I am very sorry'. The police had acted swiftly: a dastardly murder solved in less than three days. They still had to secure convictions. It was Allen's wife, Mary, who took their case forward in this regard. Still in custody, she asked to see the senior detective in the case. She wanted to make a statement. Maybe she thought being helpful would secure her release; after all, she had played no part in murder. She confirmed accompanying her husband and Evans to 'where Sandy's friend lived in Cumberland'. Sandy went into the house, and returned to the car after half an hour when both men went into the house. After ten to fifteen minutes she saw them running back to the car, and they drove off as fast as they could, saying Sandy's friend wouldn't lend them any money. After ten minutes her husband asked her for 'the sponge and soap' she had (for the children). She took his jacket off and felt the collar was wet. Sandy turned the light on and she saw she had blood on her hand. Peter (Allen) said he had caught his hand in the toilet. At Cockermouth, they got out of the car and with the benefit of street lighting she saw blood all over the front of his shirt.

Both men admitted to her that they had 'hit Jack, and he had fallen downstairs'. When they got home Peter burned his shirt. On the Wednesday morning she and Evans went to Manchester by bus, she carrying her husband's bloodstained jacket. Mary Allen knew what had happened to the knife. She said on the way back to Preston, after the murder, Evans had got out of the car and thrown it over a wall. She accompanied detectives to a spot near to St Mary's Church, Windermere, where PC George Bell and his dog, Union, searched for two hours until they found the knife, hidden under a thick pile of ivy leaves. Stephen Faulds, pathologist at Cumberland Infirmary, who carried out a post-mortem examination on John Alan West, said that cause of death was 'haemorrhage and shock caused by a stab wound in the heart, and multiple head and facial injuries'. The knife found at Windermere could have been the one used in the attack, he said.

There was ample evidence to secure convictions on both men, but still more was added when Evans's fingerprints were found in Mr West's home, and

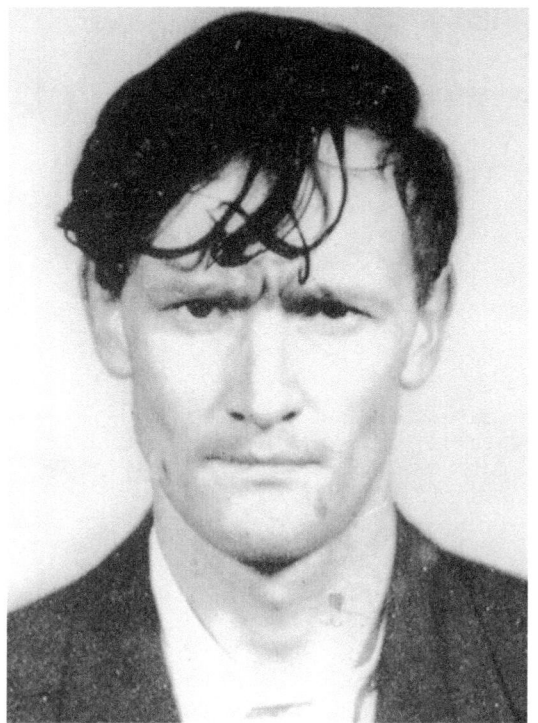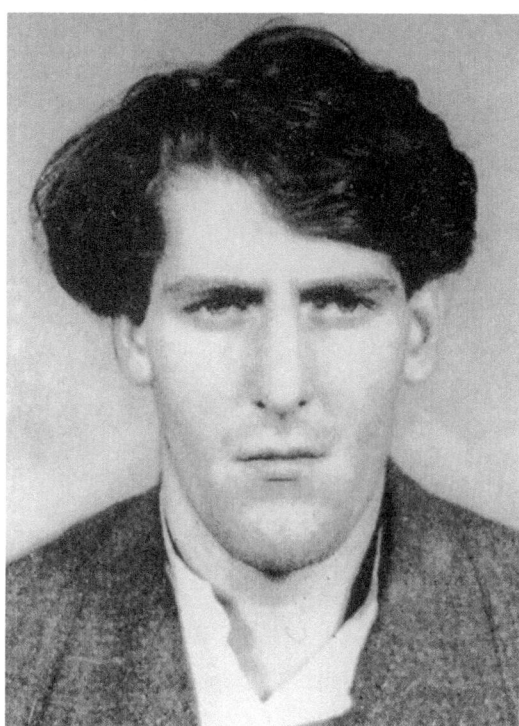

Gwynne Owen Evans and Peter Anthony Allen. (By permission of Cumbria Constabulary)

both men's fingerprints were found in the stolen car, which was recovered in Ormskirk. Blood grouping was also damning: both men were Group 'O', while Mr West was Group 'A'; there was 'A' secretion found on both men's clothing. Group 'A' blood was also found on the recovered knife and the rubber-covered tube, as well as a jacket. A director of Lakeland Laundries identified the recovered gold watch, bearing Mr West's name.

Allen and Evans appeared at Manchester Crown Court in July 1964, charged with murder and robbery. Justice Ashworth presided. While both accepted they were present at the scene of the crime, each sought to blame the other for the murder and seek acquittal for himself. Each had separate defence counsel. Evans's case was that Allen was responsible for hitting Mr West with the iron bar and that he, Evans, had shouted for him to stop. 'Peter did all the hitting,' he said. In a later statement, he said. 'Although I had the intention of robbing him, I did not intend using violence'. He said he knew Allen carried a knife, and that he had used a knife on a man in Manchester. 'It was a small wooden knife. He must have thrown it away with his clothes... The killing was all Peter's fault. I never once hit him.'

Evans told the court that Mr West had admitted him into his house and gave him a cup of tea. He then asked him for a loan of £100 and West said he would think about it. West then asked him if he would go to bed with him. Evans declined. This wasn't a surprise; he said West was a homosexual, and he had asked him before, but he had always refused. Three quarters of an hour later he heard a knock at the door. West opened it, and Evans heard a commotion at the bottom of the stairs: Allen was striking West, who ran upstairs with Allen behind. Allen had West by the throat, and was striking him with an object in his right hand. West slumped down to the bottom of the stairs where Allen continued to beat him. He, Evans, did not intervene because he 'panicked more than anyone'. When he read in a newspaper that West was dead he said to himself, 'My God, he has used a knife.'

Allen had his own version of events. He admitted he'd been in trouble before 'in connection with motor vehicles and stealing lead'. He'd been fined £20 or two months in prison in default, and hadn't paid the fine. He owed £42 in rent. He needed money. It was Evans' suggestion, he said, to visit Mr West at his home, and if he was out they would break into the house. He said he made it clear to Evans there had to be no violence, and Evans had replied, 'All right'.

When they arrived at the house, Evans got out while he waited in the car. Then Evans came out of the house and said, 'Come on in', and he followed him into the house. 'Evans was a quarter of the way upstairs. I saw an object sticking out of his coat pocket. It was like a short length of bar.' He was shown the rubber-covered tubing, and said it could have been that. He put it into his pocket to show the jury how he saw it. 'West came out of the room and said, "Who the bloody hell are you?" When I never answered he made a lunge at me. I panicked, drew back my fist and hit him in the face.' The lights went out, and he might have had 'another sweep' at him, he couldn't remember. 'The next thing I remember is seeing Evans hit Mr West with this bar effort.' Evans 'put the bar in my hand and I took a swipe at him once or twice.' Then West fell downstairs. He gave the bar back to Evans, who hit him with it a few more times and he toppled backwards. 'Evans put his hand somewhere inside his jacket and pulled out a knife and stuck it in Mr West.' Allen asked, 'What the hell did you do that for?' Evans replied, 'Jack wouldn't recognise you, but he recognised me.' They fled from the house.

An important discrepancy in the men's accounts concerned Allen's entry into the house. Evans said he heard a knock at the door and West opened it, to admit Allen. Allen's account, supported by his wife, was that he waited in the car until Evans emerged from the house and invited him to come in. Perhaps their plan had been for Evans to arrange to 'go to bed' with West, while Allen searched for money and valuables? If so, it went horribly wrong the moment West suspected what they were up to. Nor would they have been too pleased to leave empty handed, having driven all the way from Preston. Hence a hostile situation, hence murder. And when their lives were on the line, each placed the blame on the other, although whichever version was the truth or otherwise hardly mattered. They were both party to murder and robbery. As customary, the judge put on his black cap and pronounced sentence, a lot shorter than the 'hence, whence and thence' of earlier times. 'The sentence of the court upon each of you is that you suffer death in the manner authorised by law, and may the Lord have mercy on your souls.' Mary Allen, who had sat outside the court, was led away weeping.

THE EXECUTIONS

Peter Anthony Allen and Gwynne Owen Evans were hanged at 8 a.m. on Thursday 13 August 1964: Allen was hanged at Walton Prison, Liverpool, Evans at Strangeways, Manchester. The occasions were a far cry from the days of massed crowds who gathered to watch public hangings.

At Walton, on the evening before the execution, a dozen anti-capital punishment supporters distributed leaflets, and kept all-night vigil. They carried two banners, one reading 'No More Hanging', the other 'Why Take Another Life?'. About forty people were present outside the prison when Allen was hanged. As eight o'clock struck on a nearby church clock, one man stepped forward and removed his cap, and two officials for the Campaign for the Abolition of Capital Punishment, who had travelled from the West Country, stood with bowed heads. There was no activity outside Strangeways, save for the presence of a group of men and women who worked nearby, who said they were 'interested to see if any demonstration took place'.

THE VERDICT

The criminal law, amended by the Homicide Act, 1957, abolished the death penalty for murder unless committed in certain circumstances, including murder committed in the course of or furtherance of theft. Thus, Allen and Evans would have been spared the noose if they had murdered Jack West without stealing his property. The theft, not the killing alone, sealed their fate. It was a flawed law: a man who murdered and stole just one penny would hang; one who raped and murdered would not.

This was a brutal attack on a man in his home in the middle of the night, by two men who drove a hundred miles in order to steal his money. In the event they stole his wristwatch, presented to him for the hard work and loyalty he had shown the company he worked for, and then went on to obtain money – the princely sum of £10 – by presenting his bankbook at a branch of TSB. Allen and Evans were young and stupid, two hapless individuals who, when caught, blamed one another in their vain attempts to escape justice. Under today's laws they would have received a life sentence, and upon their freedom, after ten years, say, might have yet gone on to lead industrious lives. If so, would they have reflected, in later life, that that is more than they allowed Jack West to do?

15

A CAPACITY FOR MURDER

Like anyone, Stewart Lister liked a drink or two, in his case on a Sunday evening at the Carrutherstown Hotel, near Annan, where, perchance, he became acquainted with a diminutive Irishman, a debonair man with piercing eyes. Lister remembers the man well. 'He had dyed black, Bryl-creamed hair and always wore a buttonhole in his dark suit. And when it was time to pay for the drinks, he would step forward, saying, "I'll take care of that", and produce a roll of money. He was a perfect gentleman, always well spoken.' But Lister could not have known that he was also a jewel thief and conman, and if he wasn't a murderer when they first became acquainted, he soon would be.

The man was Archibald Thompson Hall (known as Roy), butler to the dowager Lady Hudson at Kirtleton House, Dumfriesshire. Stewart Lister remembers her too. 'She spoke all la-di-dah, but we couldn't believe she had a butler. She had a title, that's all.' So she did, along with a Rolls-Royce, which her butler had use of, and accommodation, which suited him nicely until the time came, as he intended, to rob her of her jewellery and disappear. For the present, he was content to live the good life: to enjoy shooting weekends on Lady Hudson's estate, to drive the Rolls, and drink at nearby Kirtleton and the Carrutherstown Hotel on Sundays.

This suited Hall, since he was not long out of prison, an institution he was familiar with throughout his adult life. Roy Hall was born in Glasgow in 1924. Intelligent, clever and resourceful, he just couldn't help himself when it came to acquiring other people's property – money, jewellery and antiques mainly. He loved the good life. As he wrote in his biography, 'I have stayed in the best hotels, drank the best wines and eaten the very best cuisine'. He also stayed in some of the most ghastly prisons, which he loathed, yet never seemed to comprehend that it was his own fault that he was a guest of Her Majesty so often.

Hall's time in prison wasn't entirely wasted. While serving his time he studied and learned about antiques, and shed his Glasgow accent for one expected of a gentleman 'in service' so that he could practise the art of deceit on gullible victims. 'He could tell you white was black,' says Stewart Lister.

One crime missing from Hall's *curriculum vitae* was violence; intelligence and cunning were the tools of his trade. And yet, at fifty-three years of age, and living the life of a lord, he became Cumbria's most notorious killer, murdering five people in the space of a few weeks, four of them with another man.

Hall was bisexual. When free, he was heterosexual (usually); inside, he partook his sexual pleasures with other inmates. One such was David Wright, whom he met in prison. Wright was in his twenties. In Hall's words, 'Emotionally there was no involvement'. Perhaps not, but when Wright was released from prison, Hall invited him to Lady Hudson's place, telling his employer he was an old friend who had just been discharged from the army. Wright was invited to work on her estate in return for board and lodgings. 'We drank her wines and spirits and had sex', wrote Hall.

Stewart Lister. (Paul Heslop)

Wright was eager to steal Lady Hudson's property and have done with it, but Hall wasn't ready. They were living the good life; they would do it, but not yet. This didn't suit Wright, who threatened to expose Hall to his employer. Then, one day, Hall noticed a diamond ring missing from a jewellery drawer. He found it, rolled up in one of Wright's socks. They quarrelled, and Wright drove off angrily, only to return in the early hours, drunk. Hall was in bed, half asleep, when he heard the sound of a gun and a bullet striking the headboard. Now fully awake, he saw Wright holding a rifle. He managed to reason with him and relieve

Archibald Thompson Hall.

him of the weapon, saying they would sort things out 'in the morning'. So he did, but not in the way Wright would have expected.

The next day Hall invited Wright to go shooting on the estate. Wright agreed, and selected a shotgun, while Hall took the gun Wright almost shot him with the previous night. As Wright fired at rabbits, Hall counted the shots. When he knew Wright had no ammunition left he told him he was going to kill him. Wright said he had been drunk. It did no good. Hall shot him in the head, then shot him again and again. The ground was too hard to dig a grave, so he stripped Wright of his clothes and any identification, laid him in a stream and covered his body with stones. He spent the following days adding ferns and other forms of camouflage, until David Wright's body was hidden from view. Lady Hudson's esteemed butler had become a murderer.

Hall explained Wright's sudden absence by telling Lady Hudson he had found employment in Torquay. But his ambition to clear her out in his own good time was thwarted when an anonymous caller exposed him as a jewel thief. The police kindly escorted him from the property. He went to London, after which, seeking somewhere quiet, he rented a cottage at Newton Arlosh, near Silloth. That November, he obtained employment as a butler again, this time in London – although he retained tenancy of the cottage in Cumbria.

Hall's new employer was a former Labour MP who had inherited a fortune, Walter Scott-Elliott. Frail and in ill health, 82-year-old Scott-Elliott lived in an upmarket flat in Chelsea with his wife, Dorothy, twenty years his junior. Hall was soon eyeing up their valuables, as well as noting the numbers of their bank accounts, which he intended to drain before going into 'retirement' abroad. First though, he intended to burgle a wealthy neighbour of the Scott-Elliott's, and to do this he needed someone more sprightly than himself. He found the man he was looking for through a long-term acquaintance, a woman named Mary Coggle.

'Belfast Mary' was a barmaid and a prostitute. She knew a man named Michael Kitto – 'a born loser', as Hall described him. But the 39-year-old was fit enough to climb along rooftops and commit burglary, so he would do. As they chatted over a drink in a pub, Kitto, impressed that Hall had secured

employment as butler to such an eminent personage as Walter Scott-Elliott, asked Hall to show him around the flat. As Scott-Elliott would have taken his sleeping pills, and his wife was thought to be at a nursing home until the following day, Hall agreed. It was the worst decision he could have made. Having shown Kitto his employer's coin collections, antiques and paintings, they were about to enter Mrs Scott-Elliott's bedroom when none other than Mrs Scott-Elliott herself opened the door. One can imagine the look on her face when she found herself looking at her butler and a total stranger, and the shocked looks on their faces when she unexpectedly appeared in the doorway. According to Hall, Kitto grabbed her and covered her mouth with his hand. Mrs Scott-Elliott, who was not in good health, slumped dead onto the floor, suffocated, or suffering a heart attack caused through fear.

How Hall must have rued his decision to bring Kitto to the flat; now they had a body on their hands. Something drastic would have to be done – and was, as events proved. The following morning, Hall told Scott-Elliott that his wife was asleep, and Mary Coggle was summoned to the flat and fitted out in Mrs Scott-Elliott's clothes, including her mink coat, and a grey wig. With Mrs Scott-Elliott's body in the boot of a car, Kitto drove north, accompanied by Hall and Coggle, who passed herself off as Mrs Scott-Elliott, and Scott-Elliot himself, too drugged up and sozzled on shots of whisky, courtesy of Hall, to know the difference. They drove all the way to the cottage at Newton Arlosh.

The next day, with Scott-Elliott either asleep or kept sedated on whisky and drugs, they drove to an isolated spot near Dunblane, Perthshire. There, as Walter Scott-Elliott slept in the car, Hall and Kitto buried his wife in a shallow grave. Then they returned to Newton Arlosh to discuss their problem: what to do about Scott-Elliott himself. They could hardly release him, firstly because sooner or later he would report his wife – and butler – missing; and secondly Hall needed time to return to the London flat to get his money and antiques. There was nothing for it but to kill him too.

The next morning, Hall, Kitto and Coggle were back in Scotland. Once again, their unwitting passenger was Walter Scott-Elliott. They drove to Blair Atholl and beyond, to Inverness-shire, looking for a suitable location to kill the old man. Near Tomich, within sight of the grand mountains of Glen Affric, Scott-Elliott asked to get out of the car to relieve himself. Kitto, in a statement he made after his arrest, described the events that followed. 'We pushed Scott-Elliott over a fence and dragged him through some bushes. We turned him over onto his back and Hall kicked him in the neck. I tried to strangle him, but the old man was stronger than expected and resisted. Roy went to the car, got a spade and passed it over the fence to me. He said, "Hit him with that", and I did'. They buried the body in a shallow grave and returned to Newton Arlosh.

Hall and Kitto then returned to London, and cleared the Scott-Elliott's home of jewellery and antiques, which Hall sold. But, back at Newton Arlosh, they had a problem. Mary Coggle had been drinking in the local pub, the Joiners

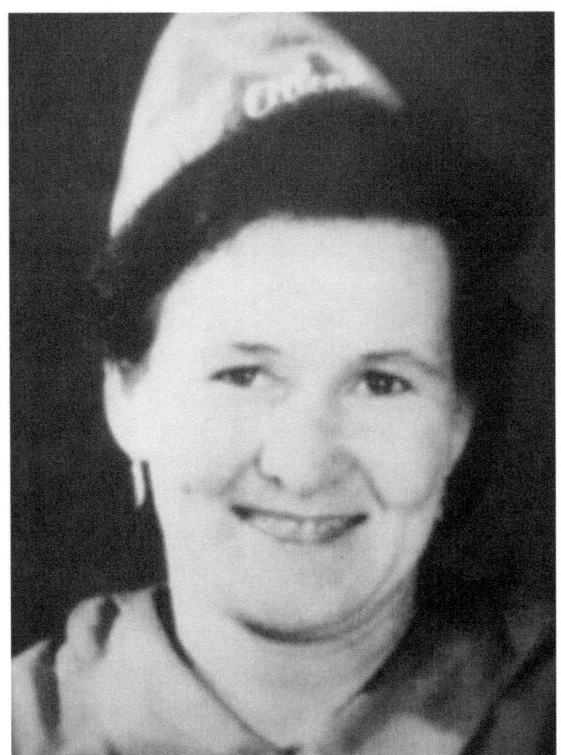

Mary Coggle. 'She had a heart of gold', said Hall.

Arms, and, in Hall's words, 'swanning around the village', still wearing Mrs Scott-Elliott's mink coat. Hall and Kitto didn't want her conduct attracting attention. Despite agreeing not to wear the coat, Coggle persisted in doing so. It would cost her her life. One evening, as Hall threatened to burn the mink coat, Coggle protested angrily, causing him to lose his temper. He went to the fireplace and picked up a poker. As he turned, Kitto grabbed Coggle's arms, pinning her to her chair. Hall struck her on the head with the poker, and thrust a plastic bag over her head and tied it at the neck. 'We sipped our brandies and watched her suffocate', he said. He regretted having to kill her; 'She had a heart of gold'.

Coggle was then dressed in men's clothing, as Hall explained, 'to make the police think it was a lesbian murder', and she became the second body to be dumped in the boot of the car. When morning came the two men again drove to Scotland to searched for a suitable place to dispose of her. In the end, they dumped her body in a stream near Middlebie. It was discovered on Christmas Day 1977 by a shepherd, but was unidentifiable. Another visit to the Scott-Elliott's flat followed, and this time everything of value that remained was taken and sold. Then, as fate would have it, Hall's half brother, Donald, was released from Haverigg Prison.

Donald was seventeen years younger than Hall, and had completed a three-year sentence for burglary. Hall despised him, regarding him as 'a dirty, unkempt tramp and a nonce' – someone who sexually assaults children. He had turned up at the door of a close friend of Hall, who, deciding he could not allow this situation to prevail, invited him up to the cottage. Donald, the 'unshaven, slovenly, lowlife scum', accepted his half-brother's invitation. On his first night at the cottage, he provided the perfect opportunity for Hall and Kitto to kill him. According to Hall (whose biographical account may not always be accurate, to say the least), Donald said a friend had showed him how to tie someone up with two pieces of string, each only 3in long. He would show them how. He cut two pieces into 3in lengths, took off his shoes and socks, lay on the floor and invited Hall to tie his big toes together. Then, looping his arms over his feet, he asked him to tie his thumbs together. 'You see', said Donald, 'I can't get out of it.' Indeed, he could not. Hall then poured chloroform onto some cotton wool, which he held over his half brother's mouth. When Donald lost consciousness he and Kitto undressed him and lowered him into a bath of hot water. Donald Hall, recently freed from one prison, was about to go into another: the boot of Hall's Ford Granada.

Another body, another intended burial – again in Scotland. But this time fate took a hand. It was 15 January 1978, and snowstorms covered Britain. Driving conditions were atrocious. At North Berwick, twenty miles east of Edinburgh, they were forced to call a halt. They could hardly afford to get stranded, and so attract the attention of the police, so they checked in to the Blenheim Arms Hotel. Unfortunately for them, the manager didn't like the look of them and called the police. As Hall and Kitto were enjoying dinner inside the hotel, two policemen were outside, checking out their car.

All might have been well if, according to Hall, Kitto had carried out certain instructions regarding their Granada's registration plates. Hall regarded the number 999 as unlucky – as he would. Kitto's instructions were to fit plates with the same number as another, identical, car, so that in the event of any check the car and number would match. This is common practice, except most criminals have the nous to alter the number on the tax disc too, so that it reads the same as the number plates – in this case, a Hertfordshire number, TUR 884R. Kitto – 'lazy, slovenly, without enough brains to be a decent criminal' – failed to alter the number on the tax disc. As Hall and Kitto were enjoying after-dinner brandies, two policemen appeared at their table with some awkward questions. They would have to be answered at the police station, and that's where they were taken. The officers had not yet opened the boot of the car, but Hall for one didn't intend to hang around until they did. Requesting to visit the toilet, he climbed out of the window, and fled. 'I wriggled through like an overweight eel'.

In blizzard conditions, Hall made a dash for freedom. All the prison terms he had served, and there had been plenty, and now five murders; he knew he would never be free again if captured. Resourceful as ever, he located the home of a taxi driver and asked him to drive him to Dunbar, saying his wife was in hospital there. The taxi driver agreed. At Dunbar Hospital, Hall asked to be driven to Edinburgh, saying his wife had been transferred there. The taxi driver agreed to this also. Alas for Hall, his bid for freedom failed at Haddington, where he was arrested at a police roadblock. Back in custody, detectives told him they had found the body in the boot of his car. They had also found seventy-six coins in their hotel room, stolen from the Scott-Elliotts' flat. Hall decided he would rather die than spend the rest of his life in prison. In his cell, he swallowed a quantity of barbiturate capsules, his 'suicide kit'. His suicide attempt failed; they took him to hospital and saved his life.

Kitto was first to talk, telling the police, 'It's an incredible story. You might not believe it, but there are another three bodies.' (There were four in respect of Hall). He admitted everything. Hall followed suit. 'For starters you had better phone Dumfries about the one no one knows about. It's a guy called David

'*Crosses mark the places where police are concentrating their investigations*'. *The body of Walter Scott-Elliott had been found near Inverness, by the time the* Evening News *published their 'bodies' guide*.

Wright. He is buried near Lady Hudson's place. I shot him in the head.' He told the police about a murder they knew nothing about, and about a body they may never have found. Both men admitted killing Mary Coggle, and cooperated fully in the recovery of the bodies of Walter and Dorothy Scott-Elliott.

Two of the murders were committed in Scotland, three in England. Consequently, there were two trials. In May 1978, at Edinburgh High Court, Hall was sentenced to life imprisonment, with a recommendation that he serve at least fifteen years. Kitto was sentenced to life without any recommendation. The following November, they appeared at the Old Bailey, for crimes committed in England. With his record, Hall was right to fear the worst. Both men were sentenced to life imprisonment again, in Hall's case the judge adding, 'Having regard to your cold-blooded behaviour and undoubted leadership in these dreadful matters, I recommend that you shall not be considered for parole during the rest of your natural life.' Even as he was sentenced, Hall wore a smart suit and carried an air of superiority. A perfect gentleman to the last.

How the Edinburgh Evening News *reported the discovery of 'a young man's body' in the boot of Roy Hall's car.*

THE VERDICT

'There is a side of me, when aroused, that is cold and completely heartless,' said Roy Hall. Indeed there was, since he had no compunction of relieving hapless victims of their valuables. For years he was non-violent, but then events took control. When David Wright almost killed Hall as he lay asleep in his bed, Hall took retribution. The death of Mrs Scott-Elliott was not intended; if Hall is to be believed, it was Kitto who killed her. Thereafter, it was premeditated murder by both men. They had to get rid of the Scott-Elliotts, or risk detection as well as lose the prize of acquiring their fortune, and Mary Coggle, who was drawing attention to them by wearing the wretched mink coat. By then, what did the life of Hall's detested half-brother matter? 'I had always known that I had the capacity for murder. I realised all that was worst in me, and once it was out there was no way to put it back.' Archibald Thompson Hall died in prison in 2002.

The focus should not rest solely on Hall. Michael Kitto played an equal part in the murders of Mr and Mrs Scott-Elliott, Mary Coggle and Donald Hall. That he was under the control of Hall seems likely, but that does not mean he was not culpable. Until they met, they were of a different breed: Hall, the clever, calculating conman; Kitto, the petty thief who was always down on his luck. It was when they came together that their lives took on a parallel course, when murder became their trade. In this regard they were two of a kind. They were given life sentences. They deserved nothing less.

BIBLIOGRAPHY

NEWSPAPERS AND PERIODICALS

The *Carlisle Journal*
The *Carlisle Patriot*
The *Liverpool Journal*
The *Whitehaven News*
North Western Daily Mail
Cumberland News
The *Westmorland Gazette*
Edinburgh Evening News
The *Daily Mail*
Illustrated Police News

BOOKS

Ashbridge, Ian Cecil, *Cumbrian Crime from a Social Perspective 1834–94*, Redburn Publishing, 1999
Klontz, Catherine, *The Embleton Murder*
Parnaby, Brian, *Murder and Retribution*
Jones, Elwyn, *The Last Two to Hang*, Macmillan, 1966
Hall, Roy & Francis, John, *A Perfect Gentleman*, Blake Publishing, 1999

RECOMMENDED FURTHER READING

Parnaby, Brian *The Netherby Hall Burglary and the Murder of PC Byrnes*, Bookcase Publishing